LEARN TO
SPEAK AND WRITE
KOREAN

Published by :
Lotus Press Publishers & Distributors

LEARN TO
SPEAK AND WRITE
KOREAN

Ravikesh Mishra

4735/22, Prakash Deep Building
Ansari Road, Darya Ganj,
New Delhi - 110002

Lotus Press : Publishers & Distributors
Unit No. 220, 2nd Floor, 4735/22, Prakash Deep Building,
Ansari Road, Darya Ganj, New Delhi- 110002
Ph.: 011-41325510, 98118-38000
• E-mail : lotuspress1984@gmail.com
www.lotuspress.co.in

Learn to Speak and Write Korean

ISBN : 978-81-8382-188-9

Printed & Published by : **Lotus Press Publisher & Distributors, New Delhi-02**

Preface

First and foremost congratulations for deciding to learn Korean language. There are around 80 million speakers of Korean all around the globe and you will join this ever growing body soon. Knowing the language will also bring you closer to the culture of Korea that has earned the epithets like "Land of the Morning Calm" and "The Hermit Kingdom". Korea is also one of the fast growing economies of the world. The pace and processes of phenoenal growth that Korea has achieved during the recent decades has made it 'Meracle on the Han River'.

Apart from helping you learn the language for the purpose of communication, which is the primary goal of this book, it endeavors to introduce the learners to the vibrant culture of the country as well. Amid the processes of globalization and Korea's own rapid growth registered during the past decade, learners of Korean language are showing a steady increase among foreigners in the recent years. The relation between India and Korea is also witnessing remarkable growth in diverse sectors, such as education, IT and tourism. After signing the recent Comprehensive Economic Parternership Agreement (CEPA), the bilateral economic as well as cultural relations between the two countries is bound to achieve new heights of growth. It is expected that this book will be a useful means to minimize the much-felt comminication gap and will foster mutual understanding between the two fast growing economic giants of Asia.

The book in your hand will guide you step-by-step through the various levels and kinds of expressions that can be used for effective comminication with Koreans in various situations of daily life. Although, the speech patterns used by a native Korean vary in different contexts depending on various factors, like, personal choice of words/patterns (styles), habits or profession, the colloquial form of speech has been used in this book, just to make it user friendly.

The book is broadly divided into four sections: the first section introduces the basic Korean phonological system (Sound system) and orthography (writing conventions). The second section includes the basic rules of the word formation processes. The second section of the book deals with the usages of language in different contexts. The situations mentioned in the book are for practical purposes and cover the dialogues that are crucial for establishing communication with a Korean speaker—both native and non-native. The third section introduces the basic Korean grammer. The fourtg section contains the reference materials, which cover wide range of vocabulary used in day-to-day life. Thus, the aim of the first part is to make you recognize and read the Korean alphabet (Hangeul); the second part will place you in the different situations using the basic language and to some extent part will place you in the different situations using the basic language and to some extent ready-made materials, sentence patterns and vocabularies. The third part will enable you to understand basic Korean grammar that are mostly used in the dialogue part of this book. The foiurth part is designed to make familiar with the basic vocabulary taken from diverse situations and contexts.

Owing to the fact that the grammatical structure of Korean language is similar to Hindi in many ways, the Hindi transliteration of the Korean sounds will certainly be a convenient and quick way for the learners who only know *Devnagri* script. To minimize the burden of remembering or pronouncing difficult words and grammatical patterns, the language of this book is kept reasonably simple which enhances linguistics competence and performance of a new learner.

I am happy to bring this effort before you, which would not have been possible without the assitance and active support of Prof. D.Y. kim, Dr. Vyjayanti Raghavan, Dr. J.M. Kim, Dr. Neerja Samajdhar, and Mr. Kaushal Kumar. I am also thankful to my student Mr. Satish Chandra Satyarthi and Mr. Gangesh Kumar for assisting me in various ways including typing and proofreading the manuscript. I am thankful to Mr. A.J. Sahgal of Lotus Press for accepting to publish this work.

The author looks forward to receiving you valuable comments, suggestions and feedbacks that could be judiciously incorporated in the subsequent editions.

Happy Learning!

September 2010 **—Ravikesh Mishra**

TABLE OF CONTENTS

SECTION-I

SECTION-II

SECTION-III

SECTION-IV

Section-I

Basics of Korean Language

Lesson 1

Introduction to Korean Language

The creation of Korea's own script 'Hangeul' dates back to 1446 when King Sejong, the 4th monarch of the Yi Dynasty (1418-1450) along with his Royal Academy scholars, who were commissioned to create a simple, easy and phonetic alphabet to replace the existing Chinese script by them, presented the Korean alphabet as 'Example and Explanation for the Correct Sounds for the Instruction of People' (*Hunmin-cheongum Haerae*). Korean people were using the Chinese characters called 'Hanja' Before the invention of Korean script. The pictorial Chinese characters were difficult to learn and speak by the koreans. It was the educated elite class who were well versed in Chinese language. The language of China, which had colonized Korea for centuries, was also considered by the Koreans as a symbol of Chinese colonialism and a loss of Korea's own cultural indentity.

The invention of the Korean script 'Hangeul' formulated by King Sejong proved to be a boon for the Koreans due to its scientific structure which helped Koreans speak their own language and subsequently assert their own identity.

Over the centuries, three consonants and one vowel dropped out of use, leaving modern Hangeul with just 24 characters that can be easily learned in just a few hours. Since Hangeul's vowels and consonants are combined to indicate a single sound (phoneme), the modern Korean alphabet is comprised of 40 characters.

In Korean, like English, the same letter can be pronounced differently. But in Korean this difference is generally rule bound and thus can be easily comperihended. The pronunciation of the letters change depending upon their portion in the syllable or word. We will study that in the following chapter. Let's first learn to read and write Hangeul.

Note: There are restrictions in covering exact pronunciations of wide range. So the nearest pronunciation has been given, especially in case of borrowed words.

These are the 14 Simple Consonants:-

ㄱ, ㄴ, ㄷ, ㄹ, ㅁ, ㅂ, ㅅ,
ㅇ, ㅈ, ㅊ, ㅋ, ㅌ, ㅍ, ㅎ

Consonant	Pronunciation	Name of the Consonant
ㄱ	Kha/Kheo ख	Khiyak (खियक)
ㄴ	Na न	Niyan (नियन)
ㄷ	Tha थ	Thigat (थिगत)
ㄹ	Ra/La र/ल	Riyal (रियल)
ㅁ	Ma म	Miyam (मियम)
ㅂ	Pha फ	Phiyap (फियप)
ㅅ	Sha श/स	Shiyat (शियत)

ㅇ	Ng ङ	Ng(अंग/ङ)
ㅈ	Chh छ	Chhiyat (छियत)
ㅊ	Chh(Strong) च्छ	Aspirated Chhiyat (छियत)
ㅋ	Kha(Strong) क्ख	Aspirated Khiyak (खियक)
ㅌ	Tha(Strong) त्थ	Aspirated Thigat (थिगत)
ㅍ	Pha(Strong) प्फ	Aspirated Phiyap (फियप)
ㅎ	Ha ह	Hiyat (हियत)

The pronunciation of almost all consonants varies depending upon its position in the given word. We will learn it in the later part of this chapter.

There are five consonants which are also used as **Double Consonants**

ㄲ, ㄸ, ㅃ, ㅆ, ㅉ

Consonant	Pronunciation	Name of the Consonant
ㄲ	क्क	Double Khiyak (सांग खियक)
ㄸ	त्त	Double Thigat (सांग थिगत)
ㅃ	प्प	Double phuyap (सांग फियक)
ㅆ	स्स	Double Shiyat (सांग शियत)
ㅉ	च्च	Double Chhiyat (सांग छियत)

Those are **10 Pure or Simple Vowels:-**

아, 야, 어, 여, 오. 요, 우, 유. 으, 이

– अ Aa

– या Yaa

– अ A

– य Ya

– ओ O

– यो Yo

– ऊ U

– यू Yu

– उ/अ U

– ई I/Ee

There are 11 Complex Vowels or Diphthongs

애, 얘, 에, 예, 와, 왜, 외,
워, 웨, 위, 의

– ए Ai

– ये Yai

– ए E

– ये Ye

– वा Wa

– वै Wai

– वे We

– व Wau

– वे We

– वी Wi

– अई/ए Ui/E

WRITING SYSTEM (STROKE ORDER)

Consonants

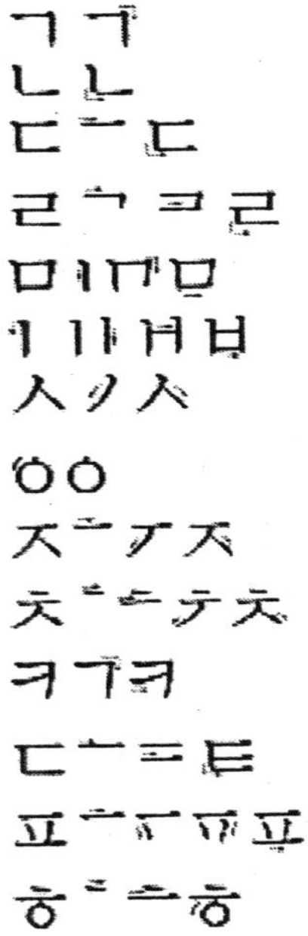

ㄱ ㄱ

ㄴ ㄴ

ㄷ ㅡ ㄷ

ㄹ ㄱ ㅋ ㄹ

ㅁ ㅣ ㄱ ㅁ

ㅂ ㅣ ㅣ ㅂ ㅂ

ㅅ ㅅ ㅅ

ㅇ ㅇ

ㅈ ㅡ ㅈ ㅈ

ㅊ ㅡ ㅡ ㅈ ㅊ

ㅋ ㄱ ㅋ

ㄷ ㅡ ㅡ ㅌ

ㅍ ㅡ ㅍ ㅍ ㅍ

ㅎ ㅡ ㅡ ㅎ

DOUBLE CONSONANTS

ㄲ ㅡ ㄱ ㄲ

ㄸ ㅡ ㄷ ㄸ

ㅃ ㅣ ㅣ ㅂ ㅃ

ㅆ ノ ㅅ ㅆ

ㅉ ㄱ ㅈ ㅉ

SIMPLE VOWELS

아	ㅇ	이	아
야	ㅇ	아	야
어	ㅇ	ㅇ	어
여	ㅇ	어	여
오	ㅇ	ㅇ	오
요	ㅇ	ㅇ	요
우	ㅇ	으	우
유	ㅇ	유	유
으	ㅇ	으	
이	ㅇ	이	

COMPOUND VOWELS

애	ㅇ	아	애	
얘	ㅇ	야	얘	
에	ㅇ	어	에	
예	ㅇ	여	예	
와	ㅇ	오	와	
왜	ㅇ	오	와	왜
외	오	외		
워	우	워		
웨	우	워	웨	
위	우	위		
의	으	의		

◆ ◆ ◆

Lesson 2

Korean Syllable Structure and Pronunciation

We have learned to write the alphabets of Hangeul. We have also learned to pronounce the vowels. But we have not learned the pronunciation of consonants. As you have read earlier, the pronunciation of consonants change according to their position in the syllable or word. Therefore, it is necessary to understand the syllable structure of Korean to learn the proper pronunciation of Korean consonants.

So, now we need to study the Syllable structure of Korean. After knowing how the syllables are formed, it would be easier for you not only to understand the pronunciation of consonants but also to read the Korean words.

In Korean, a syllable can be formed with minimum 2 letters or maximum 4 letters. Note that neither a consonant nor a vowel can come alone in the word. The sentence always starts with a consonant. If you want a vowel sound in the beginning you will have to start with 'O' which is also known as a null character.

So syllables can be formed in two ways:

Example:

ㄱ	ㅏ
ㅂ	ㅅ

= 값 (other examples: 없, 굶, 앉)

1. Consonant + Vowel (C + O)
2. Consonant + Vowel + Consonant(1 or 2) (C+O+C)

Example:

(1) (न) + ㅗ (ओ) = (नो)

(श) + ㅐ (ऐ) = (शे)

(ह) + ㅚ (दे) = (हे)

(फ) + ㅜ (ऊ) = (फू)

(2) (र) + (आ) + (म) = राम (Ram)

(ख) + (ई) + (ल) = खील (Khil)

* Notice here that final consonants are always placed at the bottom of the syllable. The final consonant is called 'Patchim'. Sometimes the 'patchim' can have maximum of two consonants but while speaking only one is pronounced prominently while the other sound is either weak or absent.

(ख) + (आ) + (प) = खाप (Khap)

(focus on practical Converstaion with minimum grammatical drills or explanations. The aim is also to enable you to read the Korean word which is the first step in order to understand the word and its meaning.

Let's now begin learning the pronunciation of consonants so that you can read Korean words. As we have discussed earlier, the pronunciation of consonants changes according to their position in the syllable or word. The pronunciation of a consonant depends upon whether it comes in the:

1. Beginning of the word
2. Middle of the word or,
3. End of a syllable (as a patchim)

So, there could be 3 possible pronunciations of a consonant. Let's have a look at the following Pronunciation Chart:-

Consonant	Name	Pronunciation In the beginning	In the middle	In the end of the word
	खियक	ख --------	ग ----------	क--
	नियन	न ---------	न ----------	न--
	थिगत	थ --------	द ----------	त--
	रियल	र --------	र/ल--------	ल--
	मियम	म ---------	म ----------	म--
	फियप	फ --------	ब ----------	प--
	शियत	श/स ------	श/स ------	त--
	अंग	No Sound	न्ग/ड़------	न्ग/ड़--
	छियत	च्छ ---------	ज --------	त --
	छियत (Aspirated)	च्छ ---------	छ --------	त --
	खियक (Aspirated)	ख (क्ख)	ख (क्ख)	क--
	थिगत (Aspirated)	थ (त्थ)	थ (त्थ)	त--
	फियप (Aspirated)	फ (प्फ)	फ (प्फ)	प--
	हियंत	ह	ह	त--
	सांग खियक	क --------	क ----------	क--
	सांग थिगत	त्त --------	त ----------	त--
	सांग फियप	प्प --------	प ----------	प--
	सांग शियत	स्स/स------	स्/स ------	त--
	सांग छियत	च --------	च --------	त --

ㄱ. ㄴ. ㄷ. ㄹ ㅁ ㅂ. ㅅ ㅈ ㅊ ㅋ ㅌ. ㅍ. ㅎ

아 -- 가 (ख)

야 -- 갸 ख्या

어 -- 거 ख

여 -- 겨 ख्य

오 -- 고 ख्य

요 -- 교 ख्यो

우 -- 구 खू

유 -- 규 ख्यू

으 -- 그 ख

이 -- 기 खी

애 -- 개 खे

얘 -- 걔 ख्ये

와 -- 과 ख्वा

왜 -- 괘 ख्वै

외 -- 괴 ख्वे

워 -- 궈 ख्वौ

웨 -- 궤 ख्वे

위 -- 귀 ख्वी

의 -- 긔 खई

Examples & Exercise for reading

By now, you must have been able to read Korean characters and syllables. Now, let's see how the words are formed using these characters and syllables. Try to read the words written in Hangeul loudly, without seeing the Hindi pronunciation.

----------------	खुदू	----------------	जूता
----------------	फादा	----------------	समुद्र
----------------	खोगी	----------------	मांस
----------------	नामू	----------------	पेड़
----------------	ओरी	----------------	बत्तख
----------------	खागू	----------------	फर्नीचर
----------------	खीच्छ	----------------	रेलगाड़ी
----------------	मोजा	----------------	टोपी
----------------	रादिओ	----------------	रेडियो
----------------	थोमाथो	----------------	टमाटर
----------------	उयू	----------------	दूध
----------------	फीनू	----------------	साबुन
----------------	फाजी	----------------	पैंट
----------------	फानाना	----------------	केला

Pronunciation Exercise

Now it's the practice time. Let's test now how good you are at reading Hangeul. The following words are commonly used for the name of places, brand, restaurants, foods and alike. You should know what most of these words mean if you sound them out correctly. The Koreanized version of sounds of the following noun is mostly borrowed from the English language and hence it differs from its original English pronunciation. The written form as well as the oral form are almost fixed and should be used accordingly. If it doesn't make sense at first, try saying it a little faster. Don't forget to check the correct English counterparts of the words provided separately. Have fun!

1. 뉴 질랜드
2. 핫도그
3. 맥도날드
4. 스트레스
5. 코카 콜라
6. 파고다
7. 헤이어 스타일
8. 한국
9. 신촌
10. 롯데리아
11. 비빔밥
12. 인터넷
13. 업그레이드
14. 학원
15. 선생님
16. 김치
17. 피시방
18. 바베큐 치킨
19. 터킬라 선라이즈
20. 바나나
21. 햄버거
22. 비디오 숍
23. 아이스 크림
24. 불고기
25. 엘리베이터
26. 필리핀
27. 러시아
28. 원 샷!
29. 테니스
30. 월드 컵
31. 택시
32. 컴퓨터
33. 나이트클럽
34. 플로피 디스크
35. 뉴욕
36. 필름
37. 텔레비전
38. 헬리콥터
39. 김밥
40. 프린터
41. 레몬
42. 소주
43. 째즈 댄스
44. 헬스 클럽
45. 오렌지
46. 노래방
47. 에스컬레이터
48. 버스
49. 멕시코
50. 치즈
51. 홍대
52. 크루즈
53. 캥가루
54. 키위
55. 인천
56. 맥주
57. 위스키
58. 슈퍼마켓
59. 테이블
60. 쇼파
61. 타이어
62. 스페인
63. 사이다
64. 껌

65. 삼겹살
66. 갈비
67. 요구르트
68. 와인
69. 뉴스
70. 스포츠
71. 현대
72. 카메라
73. 인터뷰
74. 대우
75. 부산
76. 베트남
77. 모니터
78. 스위스
79. 샐러드
80. 페인트
81. 볼펜
82. 스타벅스
83. 이태원
84. 캐나다
85. 칵테일
86. 팩스
87. 볶음밥
88. 담배
89. 아프리카
90. 샤워

1. New Zeland
2. Hot Dog
3. Mcdonald's
4. Stress
5. Coca Cola
6. Pagoda
7. Hairstyle
8. Korea
9. Shinchon
10. Lotteria
11. *Bibimbap*
12. Internet
13. Upgrade
14. Hogwon
15. *Seon-sengnim* (Teacher)
16. 'Kimchi'
17. PC *Bang*
18. Barbecue Chicken
19. Tequila Sunrise
20. Banana
21. Hamburger
22. Video Shop
23. Ice Cream
24. *Bulgogi*
25. Elevator
26. The Philippines
27. Russia
28. One Shot!
29. Tennis
30. World Cup
31. Taxi
32. Computer
33. Nightclub
34. Floppy Disk
35. New York
36. Film
37. Television

38. Helicopter
39. *Kimphap*
40. Printer
41. Lemon
42. Soju
43. Jazz Dance
44. Health Club
45. Orange
46. *Noraebang* (Singing Ro-om)
47. Escalator
48. Bus
49. Mexico
50. Cheese
51. Hongdae
52. Cruise
53. Kangaroo
54. Kiwi
55. Incheon
56. *Maekju* (Beer)
57. Whiskey
58. Supermarket
59. Table
60. Sofa
61. Tire
62. Spain
63. Cider (Korean up)
64. Gum
65. *Sam Gyup Sal* (Korean Ba-con)
66. *Khalbi* (Rib Meat)
67. Yogurt
68. Wine
69. News
70. Sports
71. Hyundai
72. Camera
73. Interview
74. Daewoo
75. Busan
76. Vietnam
77. Monitor
78. Switzerland
79. Salad
80. Paint
81. Ball(Point) Pen
82. Starbucks
83. Itaewon
84. Canada
85. Cocktail
86. Fax
87. *Phokkeum Bap* (Fri-ed Rice)
88. *Tham Bae* (Cigar-ette)
89. Africa
90. Shower

♦ ♦ ♦

Lesson 3

Rules of Pronunciation

1. Liason ('Patchim' carry-over)

a. To understand the rule of Liason, it's necessary to first understand the concept of 'Patchim'. As we have studied earlier that sometimes a consonant comes in the end of Korean syllable. In that case this last consonant is called a patchim. For example in word 람, ㅁ is a patchim. Sometimes there are double patchims in a syllable (For example, in words like 닮다, 값 etc.).

Liason is a rule that is very important in order to learn the correct pronunciation of Patchims. Let's see what this rule says:

If a 'Patchim' is followed by a vowel, its sound gets combined with the next vowel and it is pronounced as a part of the next syllable and not as an independent character.

Examples:

Word	Pronunciation	Word	Pronunciation
	खुक + ई = खुगी		मुन + ई = मुनी
	फाप + उल = फाबुल		ओत + ई = ओशी
	इप + ई = आफी		फाक + ऐ = फाके

b. If the syllable ends with a double 'Patchim' and the following syllable starts with a vowel, the first part of the double 'Patchim' is pronounced independently while the second part is carried over and gets combined with the following syllable.

Examples:

Word	Pronunciation	Word	Pronunciation
	आन्ज+आयो = आन्जायो		ईल्क+आयो = ईल्गअयो
	फाल्प+आयो = फाल्बायो		हाल्थ+आयो = हाल्थाओ
	उल्फ+अयो = उल्फअयो		अप्स+अयो = अप्सअयो

2. Nasalization

In Korean phonetic system, ㄴ,ㅁ, and ㅇ are considered as the nasal sounds. But you must remember that if 'ㅇ' is in the initial position, it is not a nasal consonant but a no sound.

When the final consonant of a syllable is non-nasal and it is followed by a nasal character (ㄴ,ㅁ), the non-nasal consonant absorbs the nasality, and is pronounced as a nasal sound.

ㄱ, ㅋ → ㅇ
ㄷ, ㅅ, ㅈ, ㅊ, ㅌ, ㅎ → ㄴ
ㅂ, ㅍ → ㅁ
} before ㄴ or ㅁ

Examples:

Word	Pronunciation
갑니다	खाप+नीदा = खामनीदा
낱말	नात+माल = नान्माल

먹는다 मक+नन्दा = मन्नानन्दा

3. Aspiration

When a consonant is followed or preceded by ㅎ [ह], it is influenced by it and gets aspirated.

ㄱ + ㅎ → ㅋ
क + ह → ख
ㄷ + ㅎ → ㅌ
त + ह → थ
ㅂ + ㅎ → ㅍ
प + ह → फ
ㅈ + ㅎ → ㅊ
च + ह → छ

Examples:

Word	Pronunciation	Word	Pronunciation
좋다	छोह + दा = छोथा	노랗다	नोराह + दा = नोराथा
생각하다	सेन्गाक + हादा = सेन्गाखाथा	입히다	ईप + हीदा = ईफीदा

4. Palatalization

When ㄷ is followed by 이 [ई], a palatalization occurs and the combination of ㄷ (थ) and 이 (ई) is pronounced as 지 [जी]. Similarly if ㅌ is followed by 이 [ई], the combination of ㅌ [त्थ] and 이 (ई) is pronounced as 치 [छी]

ㄷ (थ) + 이 (ई) → 지 [जी]
ㅌ (त्थ) + 이 (ई) → 치 [छी]

Example:

Word	Pronunciation
미닫이	मीदाद + ई = मीदाजी
굳이	खुत + ई = खुजी
같이	खात + ई = खाछी

5. Liquidation

When ㄴ is followed by ㄹ , its sound is combined with ㄹ and becomes ㄹ (ल्ल).

ㄴ (न) + ㄹ (र/ल) → ㄹ (ल्ल)

Example:

Word	Pronunciation
전라북도	छन + राफोक्तो = छल्लाफुक्तो
신라	शिन + रा = शिल्ला

◆ ◆ ◆

Section-II

Practical Conversation

Lesson 1

Basic Phrases

Hello!/How are you?	안녕하세요!
आन्यंग-हासेयो	*Anyeong-haseyo!*
I am Rahul./My name is Rahul.	저는 라훌이에요.
छनन राहुल-इएयो	*Cheoneun Rahul-yeyo.*
I am meeting you for the first time.	처음 뵙겠습니다.
छउम फवेप-केसुम्निदा	*Cheoeum phwep-kessumnida.*
Long time no see.	오래간만이예요.
ओरे-गान्मान-इम्नीदा।	*Ore-ganmanimnida.*
Glad to meet you.	만나서 반갑습니다.
मानासौ फान्गाप्-सुम्निदा	*Mannaseo phangap-sumnida.*
I have come from India./ I am an Indian.	저는 인도에서 왔어요
छनन इन्दो एसअ वास्सअयो	*Cheoneun Indo-eseo waseoyo.*
Thank You.	감사합니다/고마워요.
खाम्सा हाम्नीदा/खोमावयो	*Khamsa hamnida/khomaweoyo.*

Mention not. / Welcome.	천만이에요.
छन्मानेयो	*Chheonmaneyo*
I am sorry.	죄송해요/ 마안해요.
छ्वेसोंग हेयो/मिआन हेयो	*Chhwesong-heyo/ miyan-heyo.*
Bye.	안녕히가세요/ 안녕히계세요.*
आन्यं-गही खासेयो/खेसेयो	*Anyeong hi khaseyo/ kheseyo.*
Don't worry.	걱정하지 마세요.
खक्चंगहाजी मासेयो	*Kheok-cheong haji maseyo.*

*안녕히 가세요 is used for a person who is leaving.

안녕히 계세요 is used for a person who stays back.

♦ ♦ ♦

Lesson 2

At the Airport

While Boarding (थाप्सुंग हाल ते)	**(탑승할 때)** **(thapseung hal te)**
Rahul: Excuse me! Where can I check-in for Air India flight? *राहुलः शिल्ले-जिमान, ऐअ इन्दीया चेक इन खाउन्थअगा (थाप्सुंग सुसोगी) अदिये इस्सअयो?*	라훌: 실례지만.. '에어인디아' 체크인 카운터가(탑승수속이) 어디에 있어요? ***Rahul:*** *sillyejiman.... Air India chekhin connter-ga (thapseung susogi) adie isseoyo?*
Staff: You will have to go to gate no. 2. *छीग्वनः ई-बन छुल्गुरो खासेयो*	직원: **2** 번 출구로 가세요. ***Chigwon:*** *i-beon chulguro khaseyo.*

At The Entrance Counter (출입국 관리소에서) (छुरीप्कुक ख्वालीसो-एसअ) (churip-guk khwai-soeseo)	
Staff: Please show me your passport and immigration form. *छीग्वनः यक्वन-ग्वा फीहेंगि-फ्योरूल फोयअ छूसेयो*	직원: 여권과 비행기표 보여 주세요. *Chigwon: yeokwon-gwa phihengi-phyorul phoyeo chuseyo.*
Rahul: Yes, here it is.	라훌: 네, 여기 있어요

राहुलः ने, यगी इस्सअयो.

Rahul: ne, yeogi isseoyo.

Staff: How many bags do you want to check?

직원: 짐을 몇 개나 부치실 겁니까?

छीग्वनः *छीमुल म्यत-केना फुछिशिल कम्नीक्का?*

Chigwon: *Chimeul myeot kena phuchhisil keumnikka?*

Rahul: I have two bags.

라훌: (부칠)짐이 두개 있어요.

राहुलः *(फछिल) छिमी थू-गे इस्सअयो.*

Rahul: *(phuchil) chimi thuge isseoyo.*

Staff: Please put the luggage here and fill out these luggage tags for all your bags.

직원: 그 짐을 여기에다 놓으세요. 그리고, 모든 가방에다 이 짐표를 (써서) 붙이세요

छीग्वनः *खु छिमुल यगिए-दा नोहुसेयो. खुरिगो, मोदन खाबांगेदा ई छिम-प्योरूल (ससअ) फुछिसेयो.*

Chigwon: *kheuchimeul yeogie-da noheu-seyo. kheurigo, modeun khabangeda ye-chimphyor-eul (seoseo) phuchi-seyo.*

Rahul: Thank You.

라훌: 감사합니다.

राहुलः *खम्सा-हाम्नीदा.*

Rahul: *khamsa-hamnida.*

Staff: Have a nice Journey.

직원: 즐거운 여행 되세요.

छीग्वनः *छुल्गउन यहेंग थ्वेसेयो*

Chigwon: *cheul-geoun yeoheng thwe-seyo.*

At the Emigration Counter (이민국에서)
(ईमिंगु-गेसअ) (imin-gukeseo)

Emigration Staff: May I see your passport and boarding card, please?

이민국직원: 여권과 보딩카드 (탑승권)를 보여주실까요?

ईमिंगुक छीग्वनः *यक्वन-ग्वा बोदिंग खादु-रूल (थाप्सुं-ग्वन) फोयअ चुशिल्कायो?*

Imin-guk-chigwon: *yeokwan-gwa boarding card (thap-seung-gweon)reul phoyeo chusil-kkayo?*

Rahul: Yes, here it is.

라훌: 네, 여기 있어요.

राहुलः ने, येगी इस्सअयो.

Rahul: ne, yeogi isseoyo.

Emigration Staff: What is the purpose of your visit to Korea?

이민국 직원: 한국방문의 목적이 무엇이에요?

ईमिंगुक छीग्वनः *हांगुक फांग-मुने मोक्चगी मुअशियेयो?*

Imin-guk-chigwon: *hanguk-phangmune mokjeogi mueosi-eyo?*

Rahul: I am a businessman.

라훌: 네, 저는 사업가입니다.

राहुलः *ने, छनुन साअप्का-ईम्नीदा*

Rahul: *ne, cheoneun saeopga-imnida.*

Emigration Staff: What kind of business do you do?

이민국 직원: 어떤 사업을 하세요?

ईमिंगुक छीग्वनः *अत्तन साअबुल हासेयो?*

Imin-guk-chigwon: *eoteon saeobeul haseyo?*

Rahul: I do import-export of garments.

라훌: 옷 무역상을 해요.

राहुलः *ओत मुयक-सांगुल हेयो.*

Rahul: *oth muyeok-sangeul heyo.*

Emigration Staff: Is it your first time in Korea?

이민국 직원: 한국은 처음이에요?

ईमिंगुक छीग्वनः *हांगुगन छउमि-एयो?*

Imin-guk-chigwon: *hangug-eun cheo-eumieyo?*

Rahul: Yes. It is first time.

라훌: 네, 처음이에요.

राहुलः *ने, छएमि-एयो.*

Rahul: *ne, cheo-eumieyo.*

Emigration Staff: Well, You may proceed to the customs counter.

이민국직원: 자, 세관으로 가셔도 됩니다.

ईमिंगुक छीग्वनः *सेग्वानुरो खास्यदो थ्वेम्नीदा.*

iminguk-chikwan: *cha, seg-waneuro khasyeodo thwem-nida.*

Rahul: Thank You.

라훌: 감사합니다.

खाम्सा-हाम्नीदा.

Rahul: *khamsa-hamnida.*

(탑승할 때) While Boarding Plane
(थाप्सुंग होल ते) (thapseung-hal te)

Staff: Could you show me your boarding pass, please?	이민국직원: 탑승권 좀 보여주시겠어요**?**
ईमिंगुक छीग्वन: *थाप्सुं-क्वन चोम फोयअ चुशि-गेस्सअयो?*	***iminguk-chikwan:*** *thapseu-nggweon chom phoyeoch-usiges seoyo?*
Staff: Could you show me your passport, please?	이민국직원: 여권 좀 보여주시겠어요**?**
ईमिंगुक छीग्वन: *यक्वन चोम फोयअ चुशि-गेस्सअयो?*	***iminguk-chikwan:*** *yeokweon chom phoyeo- chusi-gesseoyo?*
Staff: Could you show your visa, please?	이민국직원: 비자 좀 보여주시겠어요**?**
ईमिंगुक छीग्वन: *बीजा चोम फोयअ चुशि-गेस्सअयो?*	***iminguk-chikwan:*** *bija chom phoyeo- chusi-gesseoyo?*
Rahul: Yes, here it is.	라훌: 네, 여기 있어요.
राहुल: *ने, येगी इस्सअयो.*	***Rahul:*** *yeogi isseoyo.*

While departing at Incheon Airport
(인천공항에서 출발할때)
(इन्छन गोंग-हांगेसअ छुल्बाल हात ते)
(Incheon-khong-hang-eseo chulbal-hal-te)

Staff: Do you have anything to declare?	직원: 신고할 것이 있습니까**?**
छीग्वन: *शिंगो हाल गशी इसुम्नीक्का?*	***Chigwon:*** *singohal geosi isseumnikka?*
Rahul: No	라훌: 아니오, 없습니다.
राहुल: *आनियो.*	***Rahul:*** *aniyo. Apseumnida.*
Staff: Your flight will be boarding at 12:10.	직원: 손님의 비행기는 12 시 10 분에 탑승을 시작합니다.

छीग्वनः सोन्नीमे फिहेंगीनुन यल्थू-शी शिप-बुने थाप्सुंगल शिजाक-हाम्नीदा.

***Chigwon:** sonnime phihengi-neun yeol-thu-si sib-bune thapseungeul sijak-hamnida.*

Staff: Your flight will depart from gate 123.

직원: 손님의 비행기는 **123** 번 탑승구에서 출발합니다.

छग्वनः सोन्नीमे फिहेंगीनन बैक-ईशीप-साम-बन थाप्सुंगु-एसअ छुल्बाल-हाम्नीदा.

***Chigwon:** sonnime phihengi-neun phek-i-sip-sam-beon thapseung-gueseo chulbal-hamnida.*

Rahul: Where is gate 123?

라훌: **123** 번 탑승구가 어디예요?

राहुलः बैक-ईशिप-साम-बन थाप-सुंगुगा अदियेयो?

***Rahul:** phek-i-sip-sam-beon thapseung-guga eodiyeyo?*

Staff: Gate 123 is on concourse A.

직원: **15** 번 탑승구는 **A** 번 중앙 홀에 있습니다.

छीग्वनः शिप-ओ-बन थाप-सुंगुनन A बन चुंगांग होरे इस्सुम्नीदा.

***Chigwon:** sib-o-beon thapse-ung-gu-neun A beon chungang ho-re isseum-nida.*

Rahul: Thankyou.

라훌: 감사합니다.

राहुलः खम्सा-हाम्नीदा

***Rahul:** khamsa-hamnida.*

♦ ♦ ♦

Lesson 3

In the Bank

In The Bank (은행에서) (उनहैंग-एसअ) (un-hengeseo)	
Rahul: Excuse me! Can I exchange from Rupee to Won here?	라훌: 실례합니다! 인도 루피를 한국 원으로 바꾸고 싶어요.
राहुलः शिल्ले-हाम्नीदा, इन्दो रूफीरूल हांगुक वॉनुरो फाक्कुगो शिफअयो.	***Rahul:** sillye-hamnida ! Indo ruphi-reul hanguk won-euro phakugo sipheo-yo.*
Staff: Sorry sir, you may change from Dollar to Won only.	직원: 고객님, 죄송합니다. 여기에서 달러를 원으로 바꿀 수 있어요.
छीग्वनः खोगेंग्नीम, छवेसोंग हाम्नीदा. यगिएसअ दाल्लअरूल वॉनुरो फाक्कुल सु इस्सअयो.	***Chigwon:** khogengnim, chw-esong-hamnida. Yeogi-eseo thalleo-reul won-euro pha-kkul su isseoyo.*
Rahul: What is the current exchange rate?	라훌: 환율은 얼가예요?

राहुलः हान्यूरून अल्मायेयो?

Rahul: *hwanyureun eolma-yeyo?*

Staff: It is 1300 Won for 1 Dollar.

직원: 1 달러에 1,300 원이에요.

छीग्वनः इल दाल्लअए छन साम बैग-वनिनेयो.

Chigwon: *han thalleo-e che on-sam-bek-wonieyo.*

Rahul: I want to change 100 Dollars.

라홀: 그럼 100 달러를 바꿔 주세요.

राहुलः खुरम बैक दाल्लरूल फाक्कुअ छूसेयो.

chuseyo.

Rahul: *kheu-reom phek thalleo-reul phakkwo*

Staff: Here it is. Please count the amount.

직원: 여기있습니다. 금액을 세어 보세요.

छीग्वनः यगी इस्सुम्नीदा, खुमैगुल सेअ बोसेयो

Chigwon: *yeogi-isseum-nida. Kheum-egeul seeo phoseyo.*

Rahul: What is the business hour of your bank? Is it open on Saturdays also?

라홀: 업무 시간은 어떻게됩니까? 그리고 토요일에도 은행은 열려 있어요?

राहुलः अम्मू शिगानुन अत्तअखे द्वेम्नीक्का? खुरिगा थायोइरेदो उन्हैंगी यल्यअ इस्सअयो?

Rahul: *eommu siganeun co-teokhe-dwemnikka? khe-urigo thoyo-iredo eun-hengeun eollyeo isseoyo?*

Staff: Normal business hour is from 9AM to 6 PM. On Saturdays, the bank is closed.

직원: 은행영업시간은 오전 9 시부터 오후 4 시까지에요. 토요일에는 쉽니다.

छीग्वनः उन्हैंग यंगप शिगानुन ओजन आहोप-शी बुथअ ओहू ने-शी काजीएयो. थोयो-इरेनन स्वीम्नीदा.

Chigwon: *eunheng-yeon-geop-siganeun ojeon ahop-si-butheo ohu nesi kaji-ye-yo.thoyoire-neun swimnida.*

Rahul: Thank You. Have a good day.

छीग्वनः राहुलः खाम्सा-हाम्नीदा. सुगो हासेयो

Staff: Thank You, Sir.

खाम्सा-हाम्नीदा.

라훌: 감사합니다.

수고 하세요.

***Rahul:** khamsa-hamnida, sugo haseyo.*

직원: 감사합니다.

***Chigwon:** khamsa-hamnida.*

◆ ◆ ◆

Lesson 4

Travel Planning

Travel Planning	여행 계획하기
(यहेंग खेह्नके-हागी)	(Yeuheng khe-hwek-hagi)

Rahul goes to a travel agency. (라훌은 여행사에 간다)
(राहुल-अन यहेंग-साए खान्दा) Rahul-eun yeuhengsa-e khanda

Rahul: This is the first time for me in Korea. I want to visit some famous places in Seoul.

राहुलः हांगन छऊमियेयो. सऊरे युम्यंग-हान ख्वां-ग्वाग-जिरूल खुग्यंग-हागो शिफअयो.

라훌: 한국은 처음이에요. 서울에 유명한 관광지를 구경하고 싶어요.

***Rahul:** hangugeun cheo-eumiyeyo..seoulre yumy-eong-han khwan-gwan-gjireul khugyeong-hago sipheoyo.*

Staff: We offer various tour packages. You can choose any one of them.

छीग्वनः उरिनन यरोकाजी सएल फेखेजी यहेंगुल जेगोंग-हेयोऊ.

직원: 우리는 여러 가지 서울 페키지 여행을 제공해요.

***Chigwon:** urineun yeoreo khaji seour phekhiji yeohe-ngeul chegong-heyo.*

Rahul: I am interested in visiting both the traditional

라훌: 저는 한국 전통 문화 유산에 관심이 있어요.

as well as the modern sites in Seoul.

그리고 한국의 현대적인 모습도 보고 싶어요.

राहुल: *छनुन हांगुक छन्थोंग मुन्हवा युसाने ग्वान्शीमी इस्सअयो. खुरिगो हांगुगे ह्यन्दे-चगिन मोसप-तो फोगो शिफअयो.*

Rahul: *cheoneun hanguk cheonthong munhwa yus-ane khwansimi isseoyo. Kheurigo hangugui hyeo-nde-jeogin moseup-do pho-go sipheoyo.*

Staff: We will show you all kinds of sites in our package tour. We will cover traditional sites like Deoksu-gung, Changdeok-Kung and Khyeonghee-gung as well as modern popular sites like Dongdae-mun, Namdae-mun, Myeong-dong, and Seoul National Museum etc.

직원: 우리의 패키지 투어에 유명한 모든 관광지가 포함되어 있어요. 역사적인 관광지로 덕수궁, 창덕궁, 경희궁, 창경궁 등이 있고 현대적인 관광지는 동대문, 남대문시장, 명동, 국립중앙박물관등이 있어요. 혼자 여행 하고 싶으세요? 아니면 그룹으로 가고 싶으세요?

छीग्वन: *उरिऐ फेखेजी थुअए युम्यंग-हान मोदन ग्वां-ग्वांग-जीगा फोहाम-त्वे इस्सअयो. यक्सा-चगिन ग्वां-ग्वांग-जीरो दक्सु-गुंग, छांग्द-क्कुंग, ग्योंगही-गुंग, छांग्यंग-गुंग, दुंगी इक्को, ह्यन्दे-चगिन ग्वां-ग्वांग-जीनुन थोंग्देमुन, नाम्देमुन शीजांग, म्यंग्दोंग, खुंग्नीप छुंगांग बांग्मुल-ग्वान दुंगी इस्सअयो.*

Chigwon: *uri-e phekhiji thu-eo-e yumyeong-han modeun gwan-gwang-jiga phoham-dwe-eo isseoyo. Yeoksa-jeogin khwang-wangjiro theoksu-gung, changdeok-kung, theungi ikko hyeonde-jeogin khw-an-gwangji-neun thongde-mun, namdemun-sijang, myeongdong, khungnip-chungang-phangmul-gwon deungi isseoyo.*

Do you want to visit alone or in a group?

혼자 여행 하고 싶으세요? 아니면 그룹으로 가고 싶으세요?

छीग्वनः होन्जा यहेंग हागो शिफुसेयो? अनिम्यन गरूबुरो खागो शिफसेयो?

***Chigwon:** honja yeoheng-hago sipheu-seyo? Anim-yeon kheurup-euro khago sipheu-seyo?*

Rahul: I prefer travelling alone. But I need a guide.

라훌: 저는 혼자 구경하고 싶어요. 가이드가 한명 필요해요.

राहुलः छनुन होन्जा खग्यंग हागो शिफअयो. गाइदुगा हान म्यंग फिर्योहियो

***Rahul:** cheoneun honja khug-yeong-hago sipheo-yo. Guide-ga han-myeong phiryo-heyo.*

Staff: Do you want to visit other famous places outside Seoul too?

직원: 서울 이외의 다른 유명한 장소도 방문하시겠어요?

छीग्वनः सऊल इवे-ऐ थारून यूम्यंग-हान छांग्सो-दो फांगमुन-हागेस्सअयो?

***Chigwon:** seoul iwe-e thar-eun yumyong-han chang-sodo phangmun-hasiges-seoyo?*

Rahul: Yes, Of course. Please suggest some famous tourist places.

라훌: 예, 좋아요. 좀 유명한 관광지를 제안해 주세요.

राहुलः ये, छोआयो, चोम युम्यंग-हान ग्वां-ग्वांग-जिरूल छेआन-हे छूसेयो

***Rahul:** ye, choayo. Chom yumyeonghan khwan-gw-angjireul chean-he chuseyo.*

Staff: When would you like to travel?

직원: 언제 가고 싶으세요?

छीग्वनः अन्जे खागो शिफुसेयो?

***Chigwon:** eonje khago sip-heoyo?*

Rahul: I would like to travel next weekend.

राहुलः थाउम छुमारे खागो शिफअयो

라훌: 다음 주말에 가고 싶어요.

Rahul: *thaeum chumare khago sipheoyo.*

Staff: We will call you tommorrow

छीग्वनः *नेईल छन्हवा थुरि-गेसुम्नीदा.*

직원: 내일 전화 드리겠습니다.

Chigwon: *ne-il cheonhwa theuri-gesseum-nida.*

Rahul: Thank you. I will be waiting for your call.

राहुलः खाम्सा-हाम्नीदा. छन्हवा-रूल खीदारी-गेसुम्नीदा.

라훌: 감사합니다. 전화를 기다리겠습니다.

Rahul: *khamsa-hamnida. Cheonhwa-reul khidari-gesseum-nida.*

♦ ♦ ♦

Lesson 5

Hotel Booking

Hotel Booking (होथेल येयाक-हागी)	호텔 예약하기 Hotel Yeyak-hagi
Receptionist: Good morning, sir. How can I help you? *आन्नेवन: असअ ओसेयो. मुअसुल थोवा थुरिल्कायो?*	안내원: 어서오세요. 무엇을 도와 드릴까요? ***Annewon:** eoseo oseyo. Mu-eo-seul thowa theu-rilkayo?*
Rahul: I would like to book a room, please. *राहुल: फांगुल हाना येयाक हागो शिफअयो.*	라훌: 방을 하나 예약하고 싶어요. ***Rahul:** phan-geul hana ye-yak-hago sipheoyo.*
Receptionist: Sure. For how many days you want sir? *आन्नेवन: म्यछिल तोंगान मुगुशील कम्नीक्का?*	안내원: 며칠 동안 묵으실 겁니까? ***Annewon:** myeo-chil tongan mugeusil keom-nikka?*
Rahul: I want to book a room for 3 days. *राहुल: सामिल मुक्को शिफअयो.*	라훌: **3** 일 묵고 싶어요. ***Rahul:** sam-il mukko siph-eoyo.*
Receptionist: what kind of room would you prefer, sir?	안내원: 어떤 방을 원하세요?

आन्नेवनः अत्तन फांगल वन-हासेयो?

***Annewon:** eotteon phangeul won haseyo?*

Rahul: I need a single room. I would prefer a room on the second floor.

राहुलः छनुन शिंगल रूमुल वन-हाम्नीदा. ई छुंगे फांगी इस्सअयो?

라훌: 저는 싱글룸을 원합니다. 2층에 방이 있어요?

***Rahul:** cheoneun singeul-rumeul won-hamnida. i-cheunge phangi isseoyo?*

Receptionist: Sure, sir. Let me check. . Yes, we have a room on the 1st floor.

***आन्नेवनः** छाम्शिमान्यो, ह्वागिनहै दुरिगेसम्नीदा. ने, ई छुंगे फांगी इस्सअयो*

안내원: 잠시만요, 확인해 드리겠습니다. 네, 2층에 방이 있어요.

***Annewon:** chamsi-manyo, hwagin-he theuri-gesse-umnida. Ne, i-cheunge phangi isseoyo.*

Rahul: Fine. How much is the room rent per day?

***राहुलः** खुरअम्यन हारूए अल्मायेयो?*

라훌: 그러면. 하루에 얼마예요?

***Rahul:** kheureomyeon har-u-e eolma-yeyo?*

Receptionist: It is 70,000 Won per day.

***आन्नेवनः** हारूए छिल-मानवन इम्नीदा.*

안내원: 하루에 칠만원 입니다.

***Annewon:** haru-e chil-ma-nwon-imnida.*

Rahul: That's fine. Please book it for me.

राहुलः ये, शिंगल-रूम-उरो येयाक-हे छूसेयो

라훌: 예, 싱글룸으로 예약 해 주세요

***Rahul:** ye, singeul-rumeuro yeyak-he chuseyo.*

Receptionist: Ok, sir. Please enter you name, address and passport number. Please sign here. Also can I see your pass-port please?

안내원: 예, 여기에 이름, 주소와 여권 번호. 비자번호를 써주세요. 그리고 여기에 싸인부탁 드립니다.. 여권 좀 보여주시겠어요?

आन्नेवनः ये, यगिये इरूम, छुसोवा यक्वन-फन्हो, बीजा-फन्होरूल सअ छुसेयो. खुरि, यगिये थुरिम्नीदा. यक्वन चोम फोयअ चुशिगेस्सओ?

***Annewon:** ye, yeogi-e ire-um, chusowa yeokwon ph-eonho, bija-pheonhorul ss-eo chuseyo. Kheurigo yeo-gi-e sain-phuthak theiri-mnida. Yeokwon chom ph-oyeo chisi-gesseoyo?*

Rahul: Sure. Can I make the payment through card?
राहुलः खादुरो खेसान-हेदो द्वेम्नीक्का?

라훌: 카드로 계산해도 됩니까**?**
***Rahul:** khadeu-ro khyesan-hedo thwemnikka?*

Receptionist: Yes. Here is the key. Your room no. is 121. This is the coupon for complimentary breakfast.
आन्नेवनः ने, यगि खी फादुसेयो. फांग-फन्हो-नुन बैक ईशि-बिल हो-इम्नीदा, ईगअसुन आछिम शिक्सा खुफोनी-येयो.

안내원: 네**,** 여기 키 받으세요**.** 방 번호는 **121** 호 입니다**.** 그리고 이것은 아침식사 쿠폰이에요**.**
***Annewon:** ne, yeogi khi phadeuseyo. Phang pheon-honeun phek-i-sip-il-im-nida. Kheurigo igeoseun ac-him-siksa khuphoniyeyo.*

Rahul: Thank you. What is the time for the breakfast.
राहुलः खाम्सा-हाम्नीदा, आछिम शिक्सा शिगानुन अन्जे-एयो?
eonjeyeoyo?

라훌: 감사합니다**,** 아침식사 시간은 언제에요**?**
***Rahul:** khamsa-hamnida, achimsiksa siganeun*

Receptionist: The breakfast is served between 6:30am to 9:30 am.
आन्नेवनः आछिम-शिक्सा यसत-शी साम-शीप-पुन बुथअ आहोप-शी फान-काजीएयो.

안내원: 아침식사는 여섯시 삼십분 부터 아홉시 반까지에요**.**
***Annewon:** achim-siksine-unyeoseot-si samsip-bun butheo ahop-si phan-kajiyeyo.*

Rahul: Thank you very much.
राहुलः खाम्सा-हाम्नीदा.

라훌: 감사합니다**.**
***Rahul:** khamsa-hamnide.*

♦ ♦ ♦

Lesson 6

Weather

Weather **(नाल्सी)**	**날씨** **(Nalsi)**
Rahul: Today the weather is very good. I really like Korean spring. *राहुलः ओनुरन नाल्शीगा आजू छोआयो. छनुन हांगु-गुई फोमल छंग्माल छोहा-हेयो.*	라훌: 오늘은 날씨가 아주 좋아요. 저는 한국의 봄을 정말 좋아해요. ***Rahul:** oneur^un nalssiga agu chohayo. Cheoneun hanguge phomeul cheon-gmal choha-heyo.*
Friend: Spring will finish in …Then the weather will be hotter. *छिन्गुः फामी ओवल-मारे कुन्नाल-कयेयो. खु हुए नाल्शीगा थवअजिल्-कअयेयो*	친구: 봄이 **5** 월달에 끝날 거예요. 그 후에 날씨가 더워질 거예요. ***Chhingu:** phomi o-wol-mare keuthnal geoyeyo. Kheu hue nalssiga theowo-jil keoyeyo.*
Rahul: So, how is the summer in Korea? *राहुलः हांगुक यरूमी अत्तेयो?*	라훌: 한국 여름이 어때요? ***Rahul:** hanguk yeoreumi eotteyo?*
Friend: Sumer is from June to end of August. It is very hot. When it rains it becomes very humid.	친구: 여름은 보통 **6** 월부터 8 월말까지예요. 날씨가 너무 더워요. 그리고 비가 오면 날씨가 무더워져요.

छिन्गुः यरूमन फोथोंग यूवल-बुथअ फार्वल माल-काजि येयो. नाल्शीगा नमू थवअयो. खुरिगो फीगा ओम्यन नाल्शीगा मुदअव-ज्ययो.

Chhingu: yeoreu-meun phothong yug-wol butheo phar-wol mal kajiyeyo. Nalssiga neomu theowoyo. Kheurigo phiga omyeon nalssiga mutheowojyeoyo.

Rahul: Which weather do you like the most?

राहुलः अनु ख्येजरूल छेइल छोहा-हेयो?

라훌: 어느 계절을 제일 좋아해요?

Rahul: *eoneu khyejeor-eul cneil choha-heyo?*

Friend: I like autumn. During autumn 단풍 is very beautiful.

छिन्गुः छनुन खाउरूल छेइल छोहाहेयो.

친구: 저는 가을을 제일 좋아해요.

Chhingu: *cheoneun khae-urul cheil choha-heyo.*

Rahul: How are the winters in Korea. Does it snow during winter?

राहुलः हांगु-गुई ख्यऊ-रून अत्तेयो? ख्यऊरे नूनी वायो?

라훌: 그리고 한국의 겨울은 어때요? 겨울에 눈이 와요?

Rahul: *Hanguge khyeo-ur eun eotteyo? Khyeoure nuni wayo?*

Friend: The winter is very cold. Sometimes the temperature falls to.

छिन्गुः ख्यऊरी मेऊ छुवयो. खाकुम ओन्दो यंगहा शिपतो-काजी तरअ-ज्ययो.

친구: 겨울이 매우 추워요. 가끔은 온도가 영하 십도 **(- 10C)**까지 떨어져요.

Chhingu: *khyeouri meu chuwoyo. Khakkrumeum on-eoga yeongha sipeo(-10C) kaji teoreojyeoyo.*

Rahul: I have seen Korean winter in the famous serial 'Winter Sonata'. So I am waiting for winters.

라훌: 저는 유명한 드라마 **'겨울** 연가' 에서 한국의 아름다운 겨울 경치를 봤어요. 그래서 겨울을 기대하고 있어요.

राहुलः छनुन युम्यंग-हान दुरामा ''ग्यउल यंगा'' ऐसअ हांगु-गे आरूम्दाउन ग्यउल ग्यंगछि-रूल फोआस्सअयो खुरेसअ ख्यउरूल खिदेहागो इस्सअयो.

Rahul: cheoneun yumy-eong-han drama 'khye-oul yeonga' eseo hanguge areum-daun khyeoul-khye-ongchi-reul phwa-sseoyo. Kheure-seo khyeou-reul khidehago isseoyo.

Friend: How is the weather of India?

छिन्गुः इन्दो नाल्शीगा अत्तेयो?

친구: 인도 날씨가 어때요?

***Chhingu:** indo nalssiga eot-eyo?*

Rahul: India has a variety of weathers. It differs from region to region.

राहुलः इन्दो नाल्शीगा आजू थायांग-हेयो. नाल्शीनुन छियंग्मादा थाल्लायो.

라훌: 인도 날씨가 아주 다양해요. 날씨는 지역마다 달라요.

***Rahul:** ineo nalssiga aju thayang-heyo. Nalssineun chiyeok-mada thallayo.*

Friend: Does it snow in India?

छिन्गुः इन्दोएदो नूनी वायो?

친구: 인도에도 눈이 와요?

***Chhingu:** indoedo nuni wayo?*

Rahul: Ofcourse, there is always snow in the northern part (like in Ladakh)which is adjacent to the Himalayan regions.

राहुलः खुरअम्यो. इन्दो फुक्पू हिमालया छप्क्यंग छियक (लादाख काथुन छियक) एनुन नूनी हांग्सांग (साह्य) इस्सअयो.

라훌: 그럼요.. 인도 북부 히말라야 접경 지역 (라다크 같은 지역)에는 눈이 항상 (쌓여) 있어요.

***Rahul:** kheureomyo.. Indo phukbu himallaya cheopk-hyeong chiyeok(ladakheu katheun chiyeok) eneun nuni hangsang (ssahyeo) isseoyo.*

♦ ♦ ♦

Lesson 7

Market

Market	시장
(शीजांग)	(Sijang)

Today Rahul has decided to go to market with his friend.

(오늘 라훌은시장에 가기로 했다.)

(ओनल राहुन-नुन शीजांगे खागिरो हेत्ता)

(oneul Rahul-neun sijange khagiro hetta.)

Rahul: I have to buy some clothes. Which market should we go?

라훌: 저는 옷을 좀 사고 싶어요. 어느 시장에 가면 좋아요?

राहुलः छनुन चोम सागो शिफअयो. अनु शीजांगे खाम्यन छोआयो?

***Rahul:** cheoneun oseul chom sago sipheoyo. eoneu sijange khamyeon choayo?*

Friend: Dondaemun and Namdaemun markets are very famous among foreigners. But Dongdaemun is nearer to our hotel so let's go there.

친구: 외국인들은 동대문과 남대문 시장에 많이 가요. 남대문 시장에 많이 가요. 가까워요.그래서 동대문 시장에 갑시다.

छिन्गुः वेगुगिन-दुरन थोंग्देमुन-ग्वा नाम्दे-मुन शीजांगे मानी खायो. थोंग्देमुन शीजांगी

***Chhingu:** wegugin-deur-eun thongdemun-gwa na-*

ई होथेरेसअ खाक्कावयो. खुरेसअ थोंग्देमुन शीजांगे खाप्शीदा.	*mdemun sijange mani khayo. Thogdemun sijangi hotheresco khakaweoyo. Kheureseo thongdemun sijange khapsida.*
(At Dongdaemun Market) **(थोंग्देमुन शीजांगेसअ)**	(동대문시장에서) **Dongdaemun sijang-eseo**
Rahul: I want to buy a jacket. Please show me some good jackets. *राहुलः छनुन छाखेसुल हाना सागो शिफअयो. छोहुन छाखेसुल चोम फोयअ छूसेयो.*	라훌: 저는 자켓을 하나 사고 싶어요. 좋은 자켓을 좀 보여 주세요. ***Rahul:*** *cheoneun chakh-eseul hana sago sipheoyo. Choheun chakheseul chom phoyeo chuseyo.*
Shopkeeper: Here it is. The quality of these jackets is very good. ***खागे छुईनः*** *यगी इस्सअयो. ई छाखेसुन छेजिरी आजू छोआयो.*	가게 주인: 여기 있어요. 이 자켓은 재질이 아주 좋아요. ***Khage Chuin:*** *yeogi isse-oyo. I chakheseun chejiri aju choayo.*
Rahul: What is the price range of these jackets? *राहुलः ई छाखेसे खाग्य-गन अल्मायेयो?*	라훌: 이 자켓의 가격은 얼마에요? ***Rahul:*** *Yi chakhesui khag-yeogeun eolmayeyo?*
Shopkeeper: This one is 1, 00,000 Won, this one is for 1, 20,000 Won and this is for 150000 Won. ***खागे छुईनः*** *ईगअसुन शिम्मान-वनिगो, छगसुन शिबी-मानवन, खुरिगो ईगअसुन शिबो-मान-वनियेयो.*	가게 주인: 이것은 1,00,000 원이고, 저것은 2,00,000 원 ,그리고 이것은 1,50,000 원이에요. ***Khage Chuin:*** *igeoseun simman weon-igo cheoge-oseun sibi-man-weon-ieyo.*

Rahul: It's very expensive. Please give me some discount.
राहुलः नमू फिस्सायो! चोम काक्का-छूसेयो.

라훌: 너무 비싸요! 좀 깎아 주세요.
***Rahul:** namu phissayo! Chom kakka chuseyo.*

Shopkeeper: First of all, you select the jacket. I will give you a good discount.
***खागे छुईनः** मन्जअ सन्थेक हासेयो. हारिन हे थुरिल-कयेयो.*

가게 주인: 먼저 선택하세요. 할인 해 드릴거예요.
***Khage Chuin:** meonjeo seonthek-haseyo. Harin-he theuril-keoyeyo.*

Rahul: The quality of this jacket is fine but I don't like the color. Actually, I like white color.

라훌: 이 자켓의 재질은 좋지만 색이 마음에 안 들어요. 사실, 저는 흰색 옷을 사고 싶어요. 그리고 디자인은 단순하면 더 좋겠어요.

राहुलः ई छाखेसुन चोछिमान सैगी माउमे आन थुरअयो. साशिल, छनुन हिन्सेक ओसल सागो शिफअयो. खुरिगो दिजाइनुन थान्सुन-हाम्यन थअ छोखेस्सअयो.

***Rahul:** I Chakhesui chejir-eun chochiman segi maeu-me an theureoyo. Sasil, cheoneun huinsek oseul sago sipheoyo. Kheurigo thijaineun thansun-hamy-eon theo chokhesseoyo.*

Shopkeeper: I will show you white color (cloths)
***खागे छुईनः** हीन सेक ओसुल फोयअ थुरिगेस्सअयो.*

가게 주인: 흰 색 옷을 보여 드리겠어요.
***Khage Chuin:** huinsek ose-ul phoyeo theurigesseoyo.*

Rahul: This cloth is very good. I will buy it if you reduce the price.

라훌: 이 옷이 아주 좋아요. 좀 깎아 주시면 사겠어요.

राहुलः ई ओसी आजू छोआयो. चोम काक्का छुशीम्यन सागेस्सअयो.

***Rahul:** Yi osi aju choayo. chom kakka chusimyeon sagesseoyo.*

Shopkeeper: Since you are a foreigner, I will reduce the price. Please give me only 1,00,000 won.

खागे छुईन: वेगुक-बुनीशिनिक्का काक्का थुरिगेस्सअयो. सिम्-मान वन मान छूसेयो.

가게 주인: 외국분이시니까 깎아 드리겠어요. 십만원만 주세요.

***Khage Chuin:** weguk-bun isinikka kakka theuri-gesseoyo. sip-man weon man chuseyo.*

Rahul: Oh...That's very expensive. Please make it to 90,000 won.

राहुल: आ! आजू फिस्सायो. खु मान वनरो छूसेयो.

라훌: 아! 아주 비싸요. 구만원으로 주세요.

***Rahul:** a! aju phissayo. khu man weonro chuseyo.*

Shopkeeper: Ok, I will pack it (for you). Please confirm again.

खागे छुईन: आल्गेसुम्नीदा. इआसुल फोजांग-हे थुरीगेसयो. तो ओसेयो.

가게 주인: 알겠습니다. 이 옷을 포장해 드리겠어요. 또 오세요.

***Khage Chuin:** algesse-umnida. I oseu! phojanghe theuri-geseoyo. to oseyo.*

Rahul: Thank you. Have a nice day.

राहुल: खाम्सा-हाम्नीदा. छोअन हारू थ्वेसेयो.

라훌: 감사합니다. 좋은 하루 되세요.

***Rahul:** khamsa-hamnida. Choeun haru thweseyo.*

♦ ♦ ♦

Lesson 8

Food

Food **(उम्शीक)**	**음식** **(eumsik)**
Rahul goes to restaurant with his friend. *राहुलः छिंगुवा काछी शिक्तांगे खाम्नीदा.*	라훌은 친구와 같이 식당에 갑니다. *Rahul-neun chinguwa kha-chi siktange khamnida.*
Friend: What would you like to eat? *छिंगुः मुअसल थुशि-गेस्सअयो?* **Rahul:** I would like something spicy. Please order something that does not have beef, pork or ham. *राहुलः मैउन उम्शीक चोम मक्को शिफअयो. श्वेजि-खोगी तोनन हैमी अम्नन गसल शिख्यअ छूसेयो.*	친구: 무엇을 드시겠어요? ***Chhingu:*** *mueoseul theusi-gesseoyo?* **라훌:** 매운 음식을 좀 먹고 싶어요. 쇠고기, 돼지고기 또는 햄이 없는 것을 시켜 주세요. ***Rahul:*** *meun eumsigeul chom meokko shipheoyo. Swe khogi, thweji khogi toneun hemi comneun geoseul sikhyeo chusyo*

Friend: Are you vegetarian?

छिंगुः छेशिक-जुइजा-येयो?

친구: 채식주의자예요?

***Chhingu:** chesik-chu-uija-yeyo?*

Rahul: No, I can eat chicken, fish and egg. Which Korean dish should I try?

राहुलः आनियो, छिखिन, सैंगसन, गेरानन मगल सु इस्सअयो. अत्तन हांगुक उम्शीगी माशिस्सअयो?

라훌: 아니오. 치킨, 생선, 계란은 먹을 수 있어요. 어떤 한국 음식이 맛있어요?

***Rahul:** anio, chikhin, seng-seon, khyeraneul meogeul su iseoyo. Eotteon hanguk eumsigi masisseoyo?*

Friend: 'Phibimphap' is most popular among foreigners. You can also try 'Dak-galbi,' 'Naengmyon' or 'saingson chiggae'.

छिंगुः वेगुगिन-दल साइए पिबिम-फाबी जेइल यूम्यंग-हेयो. खुरियो थाक्कालबी, नैंगम्यन-ग्वा सैंगसन-चिगेदो मगअफोल-सु इस्सअयो.

친구: 외국인들 사이에 비빔밥이 제일 유명해요. 그리고 닭갈비, 냉면과 생선 찌개도 먹어 볼 수 있어요.

***Chhingu:** wegugindeul sai-e phibimphabi cheil yumy-eong-heyo. Kheurigo thak-galbi, nengmyeon-gwa sengseon-chigedo meogeul su isseoyo.*

Rahul: I would like to try Dak-galbi.

राहुलः छनुन थाक्काल्बीरूल मक्को शिफअयो.

라훌: 저는 닭갈비를 먹고 싶어요.

***Ranul:** cheoneun thak-gal-bireul meokko shipheoyo.*

Friend: OK. Hello! Please give us two plates of Dak-galbi. Should we also order some drinks?

친구: 좋아요. 저기요! 닭갈비 이인분 주세요. 술도 시킬까요?

छिंगुः छोअयो, छगियो! थाक्काल्बी ई-इन्बुन हूसेयो. सुल्दो शिखिल्कायो?

Chhingu: *choayo. cheogi-yo! Thak-galbi i-in-bun hu-seyo. suldo sikhilkayo?*

Rahul: No, I don't drink alcohol. But I would like some juice.

राहुलः आन्यियो, छनुन सुरल आन माश्य-यो. हाजिमान छुसुगा छोआयो.

라훌: 아니오. 저는 술을 안 마셔요. 하지만 주스가 좋아요.

Rahul: *anio, cheoneun sureul an masyeoyo. haji-man chuseuga choayo.*

Friend: Ok. Then give us two glasses of apple juice too.

छिंगुः खुरम साग्वा जूस थू जान छूसेयो.

친구: 그럼 사과 주스 두 잔 주세요.

Chhingu: *kheureom sagwa chuseu thu jan chuseyo.*

Rahul: Should we order some more dishes?

राहुलः उम्शीगुल चोम दअ छुमुन-हाल्कायो?

라훌: 음식을 좀 더 주문할까요?

Rahul: *eumsigeul hom theo chumun-halkayo?*

Friend: Don't worry. There will be many side dishes.

छिंगुः आनियो, यांगी छुंगबुन-हेयो. यरअ-काजी फान्छान-दुल्दो मानी नाओल-कयेयो.

친구: 아니요, 양이 충분 충분해요. 여러 가지 반찬들도 많이 나올거예요.

Chhingu: *anio, yangi chun-gbun-heyo. yeoreo khaji phanchan-theuldo mani naol-keoyeyo.*

Friend: (To the waiter) Hello! Please bring me the bill.

छगियो, यंगसु-जुंग छूसेयो.

친구: 저기요, 영수증 주세요.

Chhingu: *cheogiyo, yeon-gsu-cheung chuseyo.*

Rahul: I will pay the bill.

राहुलः छेगा खेसान-हाल कयेयो.

라훌: 제가 계산할거예요.

vchega khyesan-hal koye-yo.

Friend: No, let me pay now. You can pay next time.

친구: 아니요, 이번에는 제가 낼거예요. 다음에 라훌 씨 내세요.

छिंगुः आनियो, ईवअनेनन छेगा नेल-कयेयो. थाउमे राहुल शी नेसेयो.

Chhingu: *anio, ibeoneneun chega nelkeoyeyo. Thaeume Rahul ssi neseyo.*

◆ ◆ ◆

Lesson 9

Asking Directions

Asking Directions (खिल मुक्की)	(길 묻기) (khil mukki)
Rahul: Excuse me! How can I get to Yonsei University from here? *राहुलः शिल्ले-हाम्नीदा. यगीसअ सऊल देहाक्यो काजी अत्तअखे खाल सु इस्सअयो?* Person1: Please go straight and take a left turn. You will find a church. Turn right from there. Walk for about 10 minutes. Then you will reach a roundabout. You can ask anybody there about university building. *आदमी1: ई खिरूल-तारा चूक गाशिगो वेन चोगुरो थोरा-खासेयो. ग्यो-ह्वे नाओल-खगीऐसअ ओरन-चोगुरो याक शिप-बुन गरअगाम्यन सागअ-रीगा इस्सअयो. खगिऐसअ छिनागानन सारा-मेगे मुरअ वोसेयो.*	라훌: 실례합니다! 여기서 서울대학교 어떻게 갈 수 있어요? ***Rahul:** sillehamnida! Yeogi-seo seoul dehakkyo eotte-okhe khal su isseoyo?* 사람 1: 이 길을 따라 쭉 가시고 왼쪽으로 돌아 아가세요. 교회가 나올 거예요.거기에서 오른 쪽으로 약 10 분 걸어가면 사거리가 있어요. 거기에서 지나가는 사람에게 길을 물어 보세요. ***Saram1:** I khireul tara chuk khasigo wenchogeuro कये या. thorakhaseyo. Khyhwega naol keoyeyo. Kheogiseo oreun-chogeuro yak sippun kheoreokhamyeon*

	sageoriga isseoyo. Kheogi-eseo chinaganeon saramege khireul mureo phoseyo.
Rahul: Thank You.	**라훌:** 감사합니다.
राहुलः खाम्सा-हाम्नीदा	***Rahul:** khamsa-hamnida.*
At the Crossing (सागरिएसअ)	**사거리에서 (Sagari-eseo)**
Rahul: Can you tell me the way to Yonsei University building?	**라훌:** 서울 대학교가 어디입 어디입니까? 좀 도와 주세요.
राहुलः सऊल देहाक्योगा अदी-इम्नीक्का? चोम थोवा छूसेओ.	***Rahul:** seoul dehakkyoga eodiimnikka? Chom thowa chuseyo.*
Person2: Yeah. It is right across the road.	**사람 2:** 네. 바로 길 건 너편이에요.
सारामः2: ने, फारो खिल खन्न-अ-फ्यनिएओ.	***Saram2:** ne. pharo khil kheoneophyeon-ieyo.*
At University (देहाक्योएसअ)	**대학교에서 (dehakkto-eseo)**
Person3: Whom do you want to meet?	**사람 3:** 누구를 찾으세요?
सारामः3: नुगुरूल छाजुसेयो?	***Saram3:** nugureul chaje-useyo?*
Rahul: I have to meet Prof. Kim.	**라훌:** 김 교수님을 만나 (뵙고)고싶어요.
राहुलः किम ख्योसुनि-मुल मान्नागो (फेप्को) शिफअयो.	***Rahul:** Kim khyosunim-eul manna (phepko) shiph-eoyo.*
Person3: His room is on the third floor.	**사람 3:** 아! 김 교수님의 방은 삼층에 있어요.

आदमी3: आ! किम ख्योसु-निमुई फांगुन साम-छुंगे इस्सअयो.

***Saram3:** aa ! Khim khyosu-nome phangeun samch-eunge isseoyo.*

Rahul: What is his room no.?

***राहुलः** फांग फन्होगा मुअ-एयो?*

라훌: 방 번호가 뭐예요**?**

***Rahul:** phang pheonhoga mwoyeyo?*

Person3: It's 305.

***सारामः3:** साम्बेगो हो-येयो.*

사람 **3:** 삼백오**(305)**호예요.

***Saram3:** sambego ho yeyo.*

Rahul: Thank You.

***राहुलः**खाम्सा-हाम्नीदा.*

라훌: 감사합니다.

***Rahul:** khamsa-hamnida.*

♦ ♦ ♦

Lesson 10

Making a Call

Making a Call (छन्ह्वा खल्गी)	전화 걸기 **(cheonhwa kheolgi)**
Person1: Hello!	사람 1: 여보세요.
सारामा1: यबोसेयो.	***Saram1:** Yeoboseyo.*
Rahul: Is it Mr. Kim's house? Can I talk to Mr. Kim?	라훌: 저기 김씨네 집입니까?김씨와 통화할 수 있어요?
राहुलः छगी किमशिने जिब इम्नीक्का? किम शीवा थोंग-ह्वा हाल-सु इस्सअयो?	***Rahul:** cheogi khimssine chibimnikka? **Khimssiwa** thonghwa hal su isseoyo?*
Person1: Yes. May I know who is this?	사람 1: 예, 김씨집 맞아요. 실례지만,누구십니까?
सारामा1: ने, किमशी-छिब माजायो. शिल्ले-जिमान, नुगु-शिम्नीक्का?	***Saram1:** Ye, khim-ssi chip majayo. Sille-jiman, nugu-simnikka?*
Rahul: I am Rahul from India.	라훌: 저는라훌이라고 합니다.인도에서 왔습니다.

राहुलः छनुन राहुल-ईरागो हाम्नीदा. इन्दो-एसअ वास्सुम्नीदा.	**Rahul:** *cheoneun Rajeu ragohamnida. Indoeseo wasseumnida.*
Person1: OK. Just wait for a moment I will give the phone to Mr. Kim.	사람 1: 네.잠시만 기다려 주세요. 김씨 바꾸어 드릴께요
सारामा1: *ने, छाम्शी-मान खिदार्य छूसेयो. किमशी फाक्कुअ थुरिल्केयो.*	***Saram1:*** *Ne, chamsiman khidaryeo chuseyo. Khims-si phakkwo theurilkkeyo.*
Kim: Ah! Mr. Rahul. It's really been a long time. When did you come to Korea?	김: 아 ! 라훌 씨.오래 간만입니다. 한국에 언제 오셨어요?
किमः *आ! राहुलशी ओरे-गान्मान-इम्नीदा. हांगुगे अन्जे ओस्य-सयो?*	***Kim:*** *aa ! Rajeu-si ore gan-manim-nida. hanguge eo-nje osyeosseoyo?*
Rahul: I came last Friday. How are you doing?	라훌: 지난 금요일에 왔어요. 김씨는 요즘 어떻게 지내세요?
राहुलः *चिनान खुम्यो-इरे वास्सअयो. किमशी-नुन योजुम अत्तअखे छिनेसेयो?*	***Rahul:*** *chinan kheuyoire wasseoyo. Khim-sineun yo-jeum eoteokhe chneseyo?*
Kim: I am fine. How are you?	김:저는 잘 지내요. 라훌씨도 잘 지내시죠?
किमः *छनुन छाल छिनेयो. राजु-शिदो छाल छिने-शिज्यो?*	***Khim:*** *cheoneun chl chin-eyo. Rahul-si chal chine-sijyo?*
Rahul: I am fine too.	라훌: 저도 잘 지냅니다.
राहुलः छदो छाल छिनेम्नीदा.	***Rahul:*** *cheodo chal chin-emnida.*
Rahul: Where are you staying now?	김:지금 어디에서 머무르고 있어요?

किमः छिगुम अदिऐसअ ममुरूगो इस्सअयो?

Khim: chigeum eodieseo meomureugo isseoyo?

Rahul: I am staying at Park Hotel with my friend. It's near Sincheon.

라훌: 저는 친구와 같이 파크 호텔에 있어요. 호텔은 신촌근처에 있어요.

राहुलः छनुन छिंगुवा-काछी फाखु होथेरे इस्सअयो. होथेरून शिन्छोन खुन्छए इस्सअयो.

***Rahul:** cheoneun chinguwa khachi phakh hothere isseoyo. Hothereun sinchon kheuncheoe isseoyo.*

Kim: Are you busy today?

김 :오늘 바쁘세요?

किमः ओनल फाप्पुसेयो?

***Kim:** oneul phappeuseyo?*

Rahul: I have an appointment in the morning but I have time in the afternoon.

라훌: 오늘 오전에는 약속 약속이 있어요.하지만 오후엔 시간이 있어요.

राहुलः ओनल ओजेन-ऐनन याक्सोगी इस्सअयो. हाजिमान ओहुए शिगानी इस्सअयो.

***Rahul:** oneul ojeoneneun yaksogi isseoyo. Hajiman ohuen sigkni isseoyo.*

Kim: Then shall we have dinner togather today evening?

김:그러면 오늘 저녁식 사를 같이 할 까요?

किमः खुरअम्यन ओनल छन्यक-शिक्शा-रूल काछी हाल्कायो?

***Kim:** kheureomyeon oneul cheonyeok siksareul hal kkayo?*

Rahul: Fine. Then, where shall we meet?

라훌: 좋아요.그럼 어디서 만날까요?

राहुलः छोआयो, खुरम अदीसअ मान्नाल्कायो?

***Rahul:** choayo. Kheureom eodiseo mannalkkayo?*

Kim: Let's meet at gate no. 5 of Sincheon Subway station. I will come to Sincheon.

김:우선 신촌 지하철역 5 번출구 에서 만납 시다. 제가 신촌으로 가겠어요.

किमः उसन सिनछोन छिहाछल-यक ओबन छुल्गू ऐसअ मान्ना-प्शीदा। छेगा सिनछोनुरो खागेस्सअयो.

Kim: useon sinchon chiha-cheol-yeok o-beon chulgu-eseo mannap-sida.chega sinchon-euro kha-gesseoyo.

Rahul: When shall we meet?

राहुलः म्यत शीए खाल्कायो?

라훌: 몇 시에 갈까요?

***Rahul:** myeot sie khalkk-ayo?*

Kim: Let's meet at 4.

किमः ने-शीए मान्नाप्सीदा।

김:**4** 시에 만납시다.

***Kim:** ne-sie mannapsida.*

Rahul: OK, fine. I will come by 4.

राहुलः ने, छोआयो.... छेगा ने-शी-काजी खागेस्सअयो.

라훌: 네, 좋아요......제 가 **4** 시까지 가겠어요.

***Rahul:** ne, choayo....chega ne-si kaji khagesseoyo.*

Kim: See you then.

किमः खुरम इत्तागा बायो.

김: 그럼이따가봐요.

***Kim:** kheureom ittaga phwayo.*

♦ ♦ ♦

Lesson 11

Public Transportation

Public Transportation (ख्योथोंग सुदान इयोंग)	교통 수단이용 (khyothong sudaniyong)
राहुलः ई बस छंग्न्यू-जांगेसअ बसु-रूल खिदारिन्दा.	라훌이버스 정류장에서 버스를 기다린다.) *Rahul-yi bus cheongnyu -jang-eseo busreul khida-rinda.*
Rahul: Excuse me, can I get a bus, for Sinehon from here?	라훌: 실례합니다, 여기서 신촌 가는 버스 탈수 있어요?
राहुलः सिल्ले-हाम्नीदा, यगीसअ सिन्छोन खानुन बस थाल-सु इस्सअयो?	**Rahul:** *sillye-hamnida, yeo-giseo sinchon khaneun bus thal su isseoyo?*
Person 1: Sorry, I also no idea. I will check the route map and tell you	사람 1: 죄송합니다.저도 잘 모르겠어요. 버스 노선도를 보고 알려 줄게요.
आदमी1: छ्वेसोंग-हाम्नीदा. छदो चाल मोरू-गेस्सअयो. बस नोसन्दो-रूल फोगो आल्यअ छुल्केयो.	**Saram1:** *Choesong-ham-nida.cheodo chal moreuge-sseoyo. Pheoseu noseondo-reul phogo alyeo chulkeyo.*

Rahul: Thank you.
राहुलः ये, खाम्सा-हाम्नीदा

라훌: 예 , 감사합니다.
Rahul: *ye, khamsa-ham-niea*

Person 1: Oh! There is no direct bus for Sinchon, But Bus No. 101 goes till Mapo. From there you can take Subway (Metro) Line No. 2.

사람 1: 어떻게 하지요. 여기서 신촌 바로 가는 버스가 없어요, 하지만 101 번 버스가 마포까지 가요.거기서 2 호선 지하철을 타세요.

सारामाः अत्तअखे हाजियो. यगीसअ सिन्छोन खानुन बसगा अप्सअयो. हाजीमान बेक-इल-बन बसगा माफो-काजी खायो. खगीसअ इ होसन छीहा-छरूल थासेयो.

Saram1: *eoteokhe hajiyo. Yeogiseo sinchon pharo khaneun pheoseuga eopseoyo. Hajiman bek-il-ban pheoseuga maphokaji khayo.kheogiseo i-hoseon chihacheoreul thaseyo.*

Rahul: Is Mapo close to Sinchon?
राहुलः माफो एसअ सिन्छोनी खाक्का-वयो?

라훌: 마포에서 신촌이 가까워요?
Rahul: *maphoeseo sinchoni khakkawoyo?*

Person 1: Yes, It is near by.
साराम1: ये. खाक्का-वयो.

사람 1: 예, 가까워요.
Saram1: ye, khakkawoyo.

Rahul: Ok.. then.. Shoud I take a taxi?
राहुलः खुरेयो........खुरम......छेगा थेक्सीरो खाल्कायो?

라훌: 그래요.....그럼....제가 택시로 갈까요?
Rahul: *kheureyo..... kheu-reom chega theksiro khalk-kayo?*

Person 1: There must be a lot of traffic now. So the taxi fare will be high. If you take will be high. If you take subway (Metro), you can reach earlier (then by taxi).

사람 1: 지금 이 시간은 교통이 복잡 할거예요. 그래서 택시 요금이 많이 나올거예요. 지하철을 타면 택시보다 빨리 도착 할 수 있어요.

सारामा1: छीगुम ई शीगानुन ख्यो-थोंगी फोक्चाप हाल-कएयो. खुरेसअ चीहाछरूल थाम्यन थेक्सी फोदा पाल्ली दोछाक हाल-सु इस्सअयो.	***Saram1:*** *Chigeum I sigan-eun khyothongi phokchap halkeoyeyo. kheureseo theksi yogeumi manhi naolkyeyo. Chihacheoreul thamyeon theksi phoda ppalli*
Rahul: How much would be the taxe fare?	라훌: 택시 요금이 얼마 나올까요?
राहुलः थेक्सी योगुमी अल्मा नाओल-कायो?	***Rahul:*** *theksi yogeumi eolma naolkkayo?*
Person 1: The basic fare is 2400 (korean) won. But at this time, it will be much higher.	사람 1: 기본 요금 은 2400 원 이에요.하지만 이 시간에는 요금이 더 많이 나올수 있어요.
सारामा1: खीबोन योगुमुन इ-छन-साबेक वन-इएओ. हाजीमान, ई शिगा-नेनन योगुमी थअ मानी नाओल सु इस्सअयो.	***Saram1:*** *khibon yogeumeun i-cheon-sabes-wonieyo. Hajiman I siganeneun yogeumi theo manhi naol su isseoyo.*
Rahul: How much is the Subway (Metro) fare?	라훌: 지하철 요금은 얼마에요?
राहुलः छीहा-छल योगुमुन अल्मा-येयो?	***Rahul:*** *Chihacheol yogeumeun eolmayeyo?*
Person 1: The basic price of Subway (Metro) is 1000 (Korean) won.	사람 1: 지하철기 본요금은 1000 원입니다.
सारामा1: छीहछल योगुमुन छन-वन इम्नीदा.	***Saram1:*** *Chihacheol khibon yogeumeun cheon-wonimnida.*

Rahul: Oh...Is it?
I better take Subway (Metro)
Thanks a lot for the help.

라훌: 아....그래요!
지하철을 타는 것이
좋겠어요. 도와주셔서
감사 합니다.

राहुलः आ..... खुरेयो! छीहा-छरूल थानुन गसी छोखेस्सअयो. थोवा छुस्यसअ खाम्सा-हाम्नीदा.

Rahul: *aa..kheureyo! Chi-hacheoreul geosi chokke-sseoyo. Thowa-chusyeoseo khamsa-hamnida.*

♦ ♦ ♦

Lesson 12

Appointment

Appointment (याक्सोक्)	약속 (Yaksok)
Seongmi: Hello! *संग्मी: यबोसेयो?*	성미: 여보세요? ***Seongmi:** Yeoboseyo?*
Rahul: Hello, ! I am Rahul. Are you free today evening? *राहुलः आन्यंग-हासेयो, संग्मी शी, राहुल-येयो. ओनुल छन्यगे शीगान इस्सअयो?*	라훌: 안녕하세요, .라훌이에요 오늘 저녁에 시간 있어요? ***Rahul:** anyeong-haseyo, Seongmi-si. Rahul yeyo. Oneul cheonyeoge sigan isseoyo?*
Seongmi: Oh, Today I am a bit busy. I am free tomorrow. But what's the matter? *संग्मी: आ, छनुन ओनुल चोम फाप्पायो, नेइल शीगानी इस्सअयो. खुरन्दे, वेयो?*	성미: 아, 저는 오늘 좀 바빠요. 내일 시간이 있어요. 그런데, 왜요? ***Seongmi:** aa, cheoneun oneul chom phappayo.neil sigani isseoyo. Kheureonde, waeyo?*
Rahul: Um..I wanted to watch a movie with you. Should we go for movie together?	라훌: 음, 성미씨와 같이 영화를 보고 싶어요. 우리 같이 영화 보러 갈까요?

राहुलः उम...संग्मी शीवा खाछी यंग-हारूल फोगो शिफअ-यो. उरी खाछी फोरअ खाल्कायो?

Rahul: *Um..Seongmi ssiwa khachhi yeong-hwa-rul phogo shipheoyo.*

Seongmi: Yes, good. So which movie should we plan?

संग्मीः ने, छोआयो, खुरम मुसन यंगहा-रूल फोल्कायो?

성미: 네, 좋아요. 그럼 무슨 영화를 볼까요?

Seongmi: *Ne, choayo. Kheureom museun yeonghwareul pholkkayo?*

Rahul: Let me think..I have not decided yet.

राहुलः खुल्सेयो...आजीक मोत छंग-हेस्सअयो.

라훌: 글쎄요... 아직 못 정했어요.

Rahul: *kheulseyo. ajik moth cheong-hesseoyo.*

Seongmi: What kind of movies do you like to see?

संग्मीः राहुल-शीनुन अत्तन यंगहा-रूल छोआ-हासेयो?

성미: 라훌 씨는 어떤 영화를 좋아하세요?

Seongmi: *Rahul sineun eotteon yeonghwareul chohahaseyo?*

Rahul: I like romantic comedy.

राहुलः छनुन रोमेन्थीक खोमेदि-रूल छोआ-हेयो.

라훌: 저는 로맨틱 코메디를 좋아해요.

Rahul: *Cheoneun romenthik khumedireul chuhaheyo.*

Seongmi: How about watching Korean movie? There is a good Korean movie called Speedy Scandal' running at the Seoul Theatre these days.

संग्मीः हांगुक यंगहा-नुन अत्तेयो? योजुम सऊल खुक्चांसअ छेमी इन्नअन हांगुक यंगहा 'ख्वासोक स्खेन्दल' उल हेयो.

성미: 한국 영화는 어때요? 요즘 서울 극장에서 재미 있는 한국 영화 '과속 스캔들' 을 해요.

Seongmi: *Hanguk yeong-hwa-neun eotteyo? Yojeum seoul kheuk-jangeseo chemi-ineun hanguk yeonghwa 'khwasok seukhendeureul heyo.*

Rahul: Good, I have not been able to see any Korean movie

라훌: 좋아요, 저는 아직 한국영화를 한번도 못

yet. I surely love to watch one.
राहुलः छोआयो, छनुन आजीक हांगुक यंगहा-रूल' हान-बनदो मोत-प्वा स्सअयो. कोक फोगो शिफअयो.

봤어요. 꼭 보고 싶어요.
***Rahul:** Chohayo,cheoneun ajik hanguk yeonghwareul han-beondo moth ph-wasseoyo. Kok phogo sipheoyo.*

Seongmi: Then let us watch that Korean movie.
संग्मीः खुरम, हांगुक यंगहा-रूल फोप्शीदा

성미: 그럼, 한국영화를 봅시다.
***Seongmi:** kheureom, hang-uk-yeonghwareul phops-ida.*

Rahul: What time should we meet tomorrow?
राहुलः नेइल म्यत-सीचुम मान्नाल-कायो?

라훌: 내일 몇 시쯤 만날까요?
***Rahul:** Neil myeot si-cheum mannalkkayo?*

Seongmi: The movie begins at 4:30 pm. So should we meet around 3:30 pm?
संग्मीः यंगहा-गा ने-सी साम-सीबोबुने शीजाक-द्वेम्नीदा. खुर-म्यन ओहू सेसी-सेबोबुन-चुम मान्नाल्कायो?

성미: 영화가 **4:35** 분에 시작됩니다. 그러면 오후 **3:15** 분쯤 만날까요?
***Seongmi:** Yeonghwaga nesi -sam-sip-obune sijak-doe-mnida kheureomyeon ohu sesi sip-obun cheum mann-alkkayo?*

Rahul: OK, and then let us meet tomorrow at 3:30pm in front of the Seoul Theatre.
राहुलः छोआयो, खुरम नेइल ओहू सेसी-सीबोबुने सऊल खुक्चांग आफेसअ मान्नाप्शीदा.

라훌: 좋아요, 그럼 내일 오후 **3:15** 분에 서울 극장 앞에서 만납시다.
***Rahul:** Choayo, kheu-reom neil ohu sesi-sib-obune seoul khe-uk-jang apheseo mannap-sida.*

♦ ♦ ♦

Lesson 13

Visiting a Doctor

Visiting a Doctor (उइसा-रुव फांगमुन-हागी)	의사를 방문하기 **(Uisareul Phangmun-hagi)**
Rahul: Hello!	**라훌:** 안녕하세요**?**
राहुल: आन्यंग हासेयो	***Rahul:** anyeong-haseyo?*
Uisa: How are you? What is the problem?	의사: 안녕하세요**?** 어디가 아프세요**?**
उइसा: आन्यंग-हासेयो? अदीगा आफुअसेयो?	***Uisa:** anyeong-haseyo? Eo-diga apheuseyo?*
Rahul: Now a days I have a pain in my waist.	**라훌:** 요즘 허리가 많이 아파요.
राहुल: योजुम हरीगा मानी आफायो.	***Rahul:** yojeum heoriga mani aphayo.*
Rahul: It pains even more in night. So I can't even sleep properly.	특히 밤에 더 많이 아파요. 그래서 잠을 잘 수 없어요.
राहुल: थुखी फामे थअ मानी आफायो. खुरेअसय छमुल छाल-सु अप्सअयो.	***Rahul:** theukhi phame theo mani aphayo. Kheureseo chhameul chhal su eopse-oyo.*

Uisa: Since when are you suffering with this pain?

उइसाः अन्जे-बुथअ हरीगा आफास्सअयो?

의사: 언제부터 허리가 아팠어요 ?

***Uisa:** eonje butheo heoriga aphasseoyo?*

Rahul: It is almost two weeks

राहुलः खई छूईल-चुम थ्वे-अस्सअयो.

라훌: 거의 이주일쯤 되었어요.

***Rahul:** kheoui I chhuilcheum thoesseoyo.*

Uisa: Do you do physically strenuous work?

उइसाः हिम-दुनुन इरूल मानी हासेयो?

의사: 힘든 일을 많이 하세요?

***Uisa:** himdeun ireul mani haseyo?*

Rahul: No, I don't do as such.

라훌: 아니요, 그렇지 않아요.

***Rahul:** aniyo, kheoreo-chhi anayo.*

Uisa: Have you lifted any thing heavy recently?

उइसाः छवेगुने मुगअउन छीमुल थुरअस्सअयो?

의사: 최근에 무거운 짐을 들었어요?

***Uisa:** chhoe-geune mugeoun chhimeul theureo-ssseoyo?*

Rahul: Yes, few days back I shifted slightly heavy luggage.

राहुलः ने, म्यछील-जने चोम मुगअउन छीमुल ओम-ग्यस्सअयो.

라훌: 네, 며칠전에 좀 무거운 짐을 옮겼어요.

***Rahul:** ne, myeo-chhil jeone chom mugeoun chhimeul om-gyeo-sseoyo.*

Uisa: Do you exercise often?

उइसाः उन्दोंगुन छाजू हासेयो?

의사: 운동은 자주 하세요?

***Uisa:** undongeun chhaju haseyo?*

Rahul: No, I have a lot of work (to do), so I am unable to do exercise often.

라훌: 아니오, 일이 많아서 운동을 잘 못해요.

राहुलः आनियो, इरी मानाअसअ उन्दोंगुल छाल मोत-हेयो.

Rahul: *anio, iri manaseo un-dong-eul chhal mot-heyo*

Uisa: First of all, please start doing exercise every day. Also you have to take care of the cold. You should be careful while cleaning (your room), shifting luggage and doing dishes.

उइसाः राहुल शी, उसन मेइल उन्दों-गुल हासेयो. छंसो हाल-ते, छीम ओम्गील-ते, सल्गजी हाल-ते छोशीम-हासेयो. खुरीगो थुखी छुवीए छोशीम-हासेयो.

의사: 라훌씨라즈씨, 우선 매일 운동을 하세요.청소 할때, 짐 옮길때, 설겆이할때 조심하세요. 그리고 특히 추위에 조심하세요.

Uisa: *Rahul ssi, useon meil und-ongeul haseyo. Chheongso-hal tte, chhim omgil tte, seol-geoji-hal tte, chhosim-haseyo. Kheurigo, theukhi chhu-wie chhosim-haseyo.*

Rahul: So will it get better?

राहुलः खुरअम्यन छोआ-जील्कायो?

라훌: 그러면 좋아질까요?

Rahul: *kheureomyeon chh-oajilkayo?*

Uisa: Of course. You also have to take this medicine for a week. In case there is no relief in pain, please give me a call.

उइसाः खुरअम्यो. इल्चुइल तोंगान इ-यात्तो थुसेयो. छोआ-जीजी आनुम्यन इल्छुड़ल-हूए थाशी ओसेयो.

의사: 일주일 동안 이 약도 드세요. 좋아지지 않으면 일주일 후에 다시 오세요.

Uisa: *Kheureomyo. il-c-hhuil thongan yi yakto theuseyo. Chhoa-jiji aneu-myeon il-chhuil hue thasi oseyo.*

Rahul: Thank you. I will do that.

राहुलः खाम्सा-हाम्नीदा. खुरअखे हागेस्सुम्नीदा.

라훌: 감사합니다. 그렇게 하겠습니다.

Rahul: *khamsa-hamnida. Kheureokhe hagesseum-nida.*

◆ ◆ ◆

Lesson 14

Neighbour

Neighbor (इयुत-साराम)	이웃 사람 (Iyut saram)
Rahul: Good morning! Will you please help me a little?	**라훌:** 아녕하세요! 좀 도와 주시겠어요?
राहुलः आन्यंग-हासेयो. चोम थोवा छूसी-गेस्सअयो?	***Rahul:** anyeong-haseyo! chom thowa chusi-gese-oyo?*
Neighbor: Yes. Good morning. Give it to me.	**이웃 사람:** 네, 아녕하세요. 저에게 주세요.
इयुत-सारामः ने, आन्यंग-हासेयो. छ-एगे छूसेयो.	*Iyut saram: ne, anyeong-haseyo. Cheo-ege chuseyo.*
Rahul: Thank You. I am Rahul. I am in room no. 302.	**라훌:** 네, 감사합니다. 저는 라훌이라고 합니다. 302 호에 살아요.
राहुलः ने, खाम्सा-हाम्नीदा. छनुन राहुल-इरागो हाम्नीदा. 302 होए सरायो.	***Rahul:** ne, khamsa-ham-nida. cheoneun Arago ham-nida. sam bek I ho-e sarayo.*
Neighbor: I am Seng Min. I am in room no. 35. Nice to meet you.	**이웃 사람:** 저는 셍민입니다. 35 호에 살아요. 반가워요, 라훌 씨.

इयुत-सारामः छनुन शेंग मिन इम्नीदा. 35 होए सारायो. फांगावयो, राहुल शी.	*Iyut saram: cheoneun .. Imnida. Sam-sibo-ho-e sarayo. phangaweoyo, Rahul ssi.*
Rahul: Are you from Japan?	라훌: 일본에서 오셨어요?
राहुलः *इल्बोनेसअ ओश्यस्सअयो?*	***Rahul:*** *ilboneseo osyeo-sseoyo?*
Neighbor: No. I am from China.	이웃 사람: 아니오, 저는 중국에서 왔어요.
इयुत-सारामः *आनियो, छनुन चुंगुगेसअ वस्सयो.*	***Iyut saram:*** *anio, cheoneun chungugeseo wasseoyo.*
Rahul: When did you come to Korea?	라훌: 한국에 언제 오셨어요?
राहुलः *हांगुगे अन्जे ओश्यस्सअयो?*	***Rahul:*** *hanguge eonje osye-osseoyo?*
Neighbor: It has been about 6 months.	이웃 사람: 거의 6 개월이나 되었어요.
इयुत-सारामः *खए 6 केवरीना थ्वेअस्सअयो.*	***Iyut saram:*** *kheoui yuk-keweorina thwesseoyo.*
Rahul: Your Korean is really good. Are you a student?	라훌: 한국어를 아주 잘 하시는군요. 학생이세요?
राहुलः *हांगुगअरूल आजू छाल हाशीनुन-गुन्यो. हाक्सेंग-इसेयो?*	***Rahul:*** *hangugeoreul aju chal hasineun-kunyo. haks-engiseyo?*
Neighbor: Yes. I am studying Korean at Kyunghee University.	이웃 사람: 예, 저는 경희대 학교에서 하국어를 공부해요.
इयुत-सारामः *ये, छनुन ख्यंगही देहाक्यो. एसअ हांगुगअरूल खोम्बु-हेयो.*	***Iyut saram:*** *ye, cheoneun khyeonghi dehakyo-eseo*

hangugeoreul khombu-heyo.

Rahul: Ah! Is it so?

राहुलः आ! खुरअकुन्यो!

라훌: 아! 그러군요!

Rahul: *a! kheureokunyo!*

Neighbor: Well, What do you do in Korea?

इयुत-सारामः आ! राहुल शीनुन हांगुगेसअ मुअसल हासेयो?

이웃 사람: 아! 라훌씨는 한국에서 뭘 하세요?

Iyut saram: *a! rahul ssineun hangugeseo mweol has-eyo?*

Rahul: I do business in India.

राहुलः छनुन इन्दोएसअ साअबुल हेयो.

라훌: 저는 인도에서 사업을 해요.

Rahul: *cheoneun indo-eseo saeobeul heyo.*

Neighbor: Do you live alone here?

इयुत-सारामः होन्जा सासेयो?

이웃 사람: 혼자 사세요?

Iyut saram: *honja saseyo?*

Rahul: Yes. I am alone.

राहुलः ने, छनुन होन्जा सारायो.

라훌: 네, 저는 혼자 살아요.

Rahul: *ne, cheoneun honja sarayo.*

Neighbor: If you have time, let's have dinner together.

इयुत-सारामः राहुल-शी शिगानी इस्सुम्यन छन्यगुल खाछी मगुप्शीदा.

이웃 사람: 라훌 씨 시간이 있으면 저녁을 같이 먹읍시다.

Iyut saram: *rahul ssi sigani isseumyeon cheonyeogeul khachi meogeupsida.*

Rahul: Yes. I will come to your place in the evening.

राहुलः ने, छन्यगे शेंग मिन शी छीबे खागेस्सुम्नीदा.

라훌: 네, 저녁에 셍민 씨 집에 가게씁니다.

Rahul: *ne, cheonyeoge...ssi chibe khagesseumnida.*

♦ ♦ ♦

Section-III

Korean Grammar

Lesson 1

Basic Korean Grammar

Grammar is said to be the backbone of any language. Without learning the grammar we can not even imagine of mastering any language. We have learned how to read and write the Korean words. Now you must be curious to know how the sentences are formed in Korean. So it's the high time to start learning the basic Korean grammar. Korean Grammar has a number of similarities with Hindi grammar. So if you are a Hindi speaker it's going to be a really easy and interesting journey for you. But, even if you don't know a single word of Hindi, there is no need for you to lose your heart. Korean grammar is really easy to learn for everyone who has a bit of patience and a willingness to learn it.

In Korean grammar, the sentence structure follows a subject-object-verb (SOV) pattern, but grammatical markers on words allow them to appear in different orders within a sentence without changing the basic meaning of the sentence. For example, to write the sentence - "Cheolsu reads a newspaper", the name 민수 would be given as 민수가, with the marking 민수 as the subject. The word newspaper would be given as 신문을, with the 을 marking 신문 as the object. The verb read would be given as 봅니다, with the 보 indicating to read, the —ㅂ니다 putting 보 in the present tense as a plain declarative ending. Let us see and try to make sense to the following sentence.

민수	신문을	봅니다
Subject	Object	Verb
Minsu	Newspaper	to read.
मिन्सू	अखबार (को)	पढ़ता/पढ़ रहा है

The only strict requirement of sentence structure is that the verb must appear at the end of a sentence. Speakers can omit words (even the subject) when the context is understood to the hearer. For example, to answer the question-"Does Seong Min read a newspaper?", the speaker could simply say, "rbab" meaning "Yes, (Seong Min) reads".

Ram reads newspaper in the library.

람 씨는 도서관에서 신문을 봅니다 / 봐요.

राम पुस्तकालय में अखबार को पढ़ता/पढ़ रहा है।

In the above sentence, 람 is the subject, 씨 is a honorific term of address,"[2] is subject marker, 도서관 (library) is place, 에서 is locative particle, 신문 (newspaper) is object, 을 is object particle and 봅니다/봐요 is the present form ending of the verb 보다 . You will get to learn more about it in the coming section of this book.

So there can be two types of sentences: the one ending with a verb and the other one just describing the noun. 'A (n*oun) is B (noun)*' is the most basic and common sentence pattern, in any language, to start learning the grammar with. So let us start our journey through the Korean grammar with this sentence pattern.

1. NOUN:

• **N 은/는 N예요/이에요.**

A (noun) is B (noun)

If the noun ends with a vowel, 예요 is used and if it ends with a consonant, 이에요 is used.

Ex:

• 이것은 의자예요.	This is a chair.
इगअ-सन उइजा-येयो.	यह एक कुर्सी है।
• 이것은 사과예요.	This is an apple.
इगअ-सन साग्वा-येयो.	यह एक सेब है।
• 이것은 책이에요.	This is a book.
इगअ-सन छेगीयेयो.	यह एक किताब है।
• 저는 람이에요.	I am Ram.
छनुन रामीयेयो.	मैं राम हूँ।

은/는 are particles which indicate the topic/subject of the sentence. 은 is used when the preceding syllable ends with a consonant (ex: 이것+은), while -는 is used when the preceding syllable ends with a vowel(ex: 저+는).

이/가 and 은/는 can be used interchangeably. But their use varies according to situation. Like 은, 이 is used when the preceding syllable ends with a consonant (ex: 이것+이), while 가 is used when the preceding syllable ends with a vowel(ex: 저+가 which becomes 제가).

Ex:

• 람씨가 의사입니다.	Mr. Ram is a doctor.
राम-शीगा उइसा-इम्नीदा.	मि. राम एक डॉक्टर हैं।
• 람씨는 의사입니다.	Mr. Ram is a doctor.
राम-शीनुन उइसा-इम्नीदा.	मि. राम एक डॉक्टर हैं।

Both the above sentences are similar and grammatically correct but nuance may differ. '씨 (शी)' is a respective term of address that can be added at the end of someone's name. It can be used with the first name or full name, regardless of sex.

사람 is added after the country's name to indicate one's nationality. And 어 is added after country's name to indicate the language of that country.

Ex:

Country	Nationality	Languaage
• 한국 **हांगुक** (Korea)	한국 사람 **हांगुक साराम** (Korean person)	한국어 **हान्गुगअ** (Korean Language)
• 일본 **ईल्बोन** (Japan)	일본 사람 **ईल्बोन साराम** (Japanese person)	일본어 **ईल्बोनअ** (Japanese Language)

The objective marker '-을/를'

The marker '을/를' is attached to a Noun to indicate the direct object of a transitive verb. '-를 ' is used after a vowel while '을 ' is used after a consonant.

• 생일파티를 했어요.	We had a birthday party.
सेंगील फाथेरुल हेस्सअयो.	हम लोगों ने जन्मदिन की पार्टी मनाई।
• 점심을 먹었어요.	I ate lunch.
छम्सीमुल मगस्सअयो.	मैंने लंच किया
• 친구를 만나겠어요.	I will meet my friend.
छींग-रुल मान्ना-गेस्सअयो.	मैं अपने दोस्त से मिलूंगा।
• 책을 샀어요.	I bought a book.
छेगुल सास्सअयो.	मैंने एक किताब खरीदी।

In most of cases, a subject is simply not said in Korean.

A: 개가 누구를 물었어요?	Who did the dog bite?
खेगा नुगुरुल मुरअस्सअयो?	*कुत्ते ने किसे काटा?*
B: 개가 사람을 물었어요	(It) bite a person.
सारामुल मुरअस्सअयो?	*इसने आदमी को काटा है।*

- 도 (-दो)

It is a particle with the meaning of 'also/ too.' It can come after noun and may also be attached to the end of other particles.

Ex:

• 사과를 먹어요.	I eat apple.
साग्वारुल मगअयो.	मैं सेब खाता हूँ।
• 수박도 먹어요.	I eat melon too.
सुबाक-दो मगअयो.	मैं तरबूज भी खाता हूँ।
• 공책을 샀어요	I bought a notebook.

खोंग-छेगुल सास्सअयो.	मैंने नोटबुक खरीदी।
• 연필도 샀어요.	I also bought a pencil.
यन्फिल-दो सास्सअयो.	मैंने पेंसिल भी खरीदी।
• 친구도 만났어요.	I met my frind also.
छीन्गुदो मान्नास्सअयो.	मैं दोस्त से भी मिला
• 라메스도 인도 사람이에요.	Ramesh is also an Indian.
रमेश-दो इन्दो-साराम-इएयो.	रमेश भी एक भारतीय है।
• 저도 한국말을 해요.	I too speak Korean.
छदो हांगुंग-मारुल हेयो.	मैं भी कोरियन बोलता हूँ।

1. VERB

Korean verbs are also known in English as "action verbs" or "dynamic verbs" to distinguish them from adjectives, which are also known as "descriptive verbs". Examples of action/dynamic verbs are 하다 (to do) and 가다 (to go) which constitute an action or movement as opposed to descriptive verbs such as 예쁘다 (to be beautiful). Action verbs denote an action by the subject while the descriptive verbs describe the qualities of the subject.

Unlike most of the European languages, Korean does not conjugate verbs using agreement with the subject, and nouns have no gender. Instead, verb conjugations depend upon the verb tense, aspect, mood, and the social relation between the speaker, the subjects, and the listeners. For example, different endings are used depending on the speaker's relation with their subject or audience. Politeness is a critical part of Korean language and Korean culture; therefore, when talking to someone esteemed, the correct verb ending must be chosen to indicate the proper respect.

We can categorize Verb endings into two types: Formal and Plain.

Ex:-

Formal Ending – ㅂ니다 / 습니다

Plain Ending – 어요 / 아요

Formal Ending is used in writings or speaking with older people or on formal occasions while Plain ending is used in most of the practical conversations. Plain speech style is most widely used in Korea. Speakers can use this style when they wish to talk politely, but informally, in any situation. We will mostly use this style in this book.

A Note on Conjugation

All Korean verbs end with 다 . Before attaching any sentence ending we remove the '다 ' and add the ending to the verb root only.

Verb	Verb Root	Sentence Ending	Conjugated Verb
먹다	먹	-어요	먹어요.
가다	가	-ㄹ까요?	갈까요?

A Note on Traditional Vowel Classification

Before starting learning tense endings, it is necessary to learn the Traditional vowel classification in Korean language.

Traditionally, vowels are classified into three categories, that are *yang* (bright), *yin* (dark), and neutral. This classification came into Korean language from Chinese traditions. It is very important to learn it, for it will be used when we learn conjugation of predicates and some phonological aspects of Korean. The classification also follows the vowel-harmony phenomena that Korean has, as a member of Altaic language family. The classification is as follows:

Yang (bright) — ㅏ and ㅗ series (ㅏ, ㅑ, ㅗ, ㅛ, ㅘ)

Yin (dark) — ㅓ and ㅜ series (ㅓ, ㅕ, ㅜ, ㅠ, ㅝ)

Neutral — 으 and 이

3. TENSE

Present Tense 아요/어요 (आयो/अयो)

It is the present tense verb ending. It is used with both action and descriptive verbs. If the last vowel of the verb is 아 or 오 then 요 is used and if the last vowel is 어 or 우 then is used.

Note: If the word ends with vowel 아 , just 요 will be added.

Explanation:

가다 (To go) : 가요

In fact, 가다 → 가요 is a contraction [가 + -아요 (가아요) → 가요]

Note: 하다 verbs and adjectives are rather peculiar. For them, -여요 is assumed instead of -아요 . All the -하다 stems with no exception appear as -해요 .

(1) '아요' form: (आयो)

This is used when the last vowel of the verb root is a bright vowel ('ㅏ' or 'ㅗ')

알다 ; 알 +	아요	--> 알아요
좋다 ; 좋 +	아요	--> 좋아요
가다 ; 가 +	아요	--> 가아요 --> 가요 **(Contraction)**
오다 ; 오 +	아요	--> 오아요 --> 와요 **(Contraction)**

(2) '어요' form: (अयो)

This is used after any other last vowel of the verb stem except for the '아요' and '여요' cases.

있다 ; 있 +	어요	--> 있어요
먹다 ; 먹 +	어요	--> 먹어요
없다 ` 없 +	어요	--> 없어요

(3) '여요' form:

This is used after a '하다` verb.

공부하다 ; 공부하 +	여요	--> 공부하여요 --> 공부해요 **(contraction)**
좋아하다 : 좋아하 +	여요	--> 좋아하여요 --> 좋아해요 **(contraction)**
노래하다 ; 노래하 +	여요	--> 노래하여요 --> 노래해요 **(contraction)**

Example Sentences:

- 이 책이 좋아요. — This book is good. यह किताब अच्छी है।
- 그는 한국에 가요. — He is going to Korea. वह कोरिया जा रहा है।
- 저는 밥을 먹어요. — I eat rice. मैं खाना खाता हूँ
- 볼펜이 없어요. — I don't have a pen. मेरे पास कलम नहीं है।
- 김치를 좋아해요. — I like Kimchi. मैं किमची पंसद करता हूँ।

Making Interrogative Sentences '-아(어/여)요?'

It is very simple to make an interrogative sentence in Korean. There is no subject-verb inversion as in English. You can make Yes/No question with rising intonation at the end of the sentence. For wh-questions (questions using what, where, who, why etc.), you should use interrogatives such as'어디 (where)' and '무엇 (what)'.

- 의자가 책상 옆에 있어요 — There is a chair beside the desk.
  उइजागा छेक्सांग-यफे इस्सअयो — कुर्सी मेज के बगल में है।
- 의자가 책상 옆에 있어요? — Is there a chair beside the desk?
  उइजागा छेक्सांग-यफे इस्सअयो? — क्या कुर्सी मेज के बगल में है?
- 의자가 어디에 있어요? — Where is the chair?

उइजागा अदीए इस्सअयो?	कुर्सी कहाँ पर है?
• 이것은 맥주예요.	This is beer.
इगसन मेक्चूयेयो.	यह मेक्चू (बीयर) है।
• 이것은 맥주예요?	Is this beer?
इगसन मेक्चूयेयो?	क्या यह मेक्चू (बीयर) है?
• 학교에서 무엇을 해요?	What do you do in school?
हाक्यो-एसअ मुअसुल हेयो?	तुम स्कूल में क्या करते हो?
• 학교에서 공부를 해요.	I study in school.
हाक्यो-एसअ खोम्बु-रुल हेयो.	मैं स्कूल में पढ़ता हूँ।

PAST TENSE

- 았어요/었어요 (आ'स्सअयो/अस्सअयो)

It is past tense verb ending. All the rules are same as 아요/어요 ending. Also remember the exception of 하다 verbs.

(1) -았- (आत)

When the final vowel of the verb stem is 'ㅏ,ㅗ', it takes '-았-'

많다: 많 + 았어요 -> 많았어요.

좋다: 좋 + 았어요. -> 좋았어요.

만나다: 만나 + 았어요

-> 만나았어요. -> 만났어요.

오다: 오 + 았어요

오았어요. -> 왔어요.

(2) 었 (अत)

When the final vowel of the verb stem is any other vowel like 'ㅓ, ㅜ, ㅡ, ㅣ, it takes '-았-'.

먹다: 먹 + 었어요-> 먹었어요.

읽다: 읽 + 었어요. -> 읽었어요.

가르치다: + 가르치 + 었어요 -> 가르치었어요 > 가르쳤어요.

찍다: 찍 + 었어요-> 찍었어요.

(3) 였(यत)

When the verb is a '하다 ' verb, it takes '-았-'.

산책하다: 산책하 + 였어요

> 산책하였어요. -> 산책했어요.

기뻐하다: 기뻐하 + 였어요

-> 기뻐하였어요. -> 기뻐했어요.

가르치다:가르치 +였어요 -> 가르쳤어요.

Example Sentences:

• 이 책이 좋았어요.	This book was good.
इ छेगी छोआ-स्मअयो.	यह किताब अच्छी थी।
• 그는 한국에 갔어요.	He went to Korea.
खुनुन हांगुगे खा-स्सअयो.	वह कोरिया गया।
• 저는 밥을 먹었어요.	I ate rice.
छनुन फाबुल मगअ-स्सअयो.	मैंने खाना खाया।
• 볼펜이 없었어요.	I didn't have a pen.
फोल्फेनी अप्सअ-सयो.	मेरे पास कलम नहीं थी।

• 김치를 좋아했어요.	I liked 'Kimchi'.
किमछीरुल छोआ-हेस्सअयो.	मैं किमची पसंद करता था।

FUTURE TENSE

a. '-겠-':guess/conjecture (गेत)

This pre-ending -겠- is used for expressing the speaker's conjecture or supposition or for asking intention of the person spoken to in a polite request.

• 요즘 많이 바쁘겠어요.	I think you must be busy these days.
योजुम मानी फापु-गेस्सअयो	लगता है आजकल आप काफी व्यस्त हैं।
• 뭘 드시겠어요?	What will you eat?
मुअल थुसी-गेस्सअयो?	आप क्या खाएंगे?
• 언제 오겠어요?	When will you come?
अन्जे ओ-गेस्सअयो?	आप कब आएँगे?
• 내일 다섯 시에 가겠어요.	I will go at 5 o'clock tomorrow.
नेइल थासत सीए खा-गेस्सअयो।	मैं कल 5 बजे जाऊंगा।

b. '-(으)ㄹ 거에요 ':will (उल कयेयो)

This pattern is used to express an action which is going to take place in the future. This grammar pattern is most widely used in making sentences with future tense. It is more popular than '-겠- ' pattern in practical conversations.

If the verb stem ends in a vowel, we add -ㄹ 거에요 with the verb root.

• 안나씨, 내일 뭐 할 거에요?	Anna, what will you do tomorrow?
अन्ना शी, नेईल मुअसल हाल-कयेयो?	अन्ना, आप कल क्या करेंगे?
• 저는 내일 영화를 볼 거에요.	I will watch a movie tomorrow.
छनुन नेईल यंगह्वारुल फोल-कयेयो.	मैं कल एक फिल्म देखूंगा।
• 이번 방학에는 뭘 하실 거에요?	What will you do this vacation?
इ-बन फांग-हागेनुन मुअल हासील-कएयो?	आप इन छुट्टियों में क्या करेंगे?
• 김 씨는 다음 달에 한국에 갈 거에요.	Mr. Kim will go to Korea next month.
किम सीनुन थाउम दारे हांगुगे खाल-कएयो.	मि. किम अगले महीने कोरिया जाएंगे।
• 일요일에 친구를 만날 거에요.	I will meet my friend on Sunday.
इर्योइरे छींगु-रुल मान्नाल-कएयो.	मैं रविवार को अपने दोस्त से मिलूंगा।

If the verb stem ends in a consonant, we add –을 거에요 with the verb root.

• 지금 점심을먹을 거예요?	Will you have lunch now?
छीगुम छम्शीमुल मगल कयेयो?	क्या आप अभी लंच करेंगें?
• 아니오, 30분 후에 먹을 거예요.	No, I will have it in 30 minutes.

आनिओ, साम सीप बुन हुए मगुल कयेयो.	नहीं मैं आधे घंटे बाद करूंगा।
• 저는 내일 한복을 입을 거예요.	I will wear 'Hanbok' (Traditional korean dress) tomorrow.
छनुन नेईल हान्बोगुल इबुल कयेयो.	मैं कल हान्बोक (कोरियाई पारंपरिक पोशाक) पहनूंगा।
• 모한 씨는 음악을 들을 거에요.	Mr. Mohan will listen to music.
मोहन सीनुन उमागुल थुरुल कएयो.	मि. मोहन संगीत सुनेंगे।
• 어디에서앉을 거에요?	Where will you sit?
अदी-एसअ आन्जुल कएयो?	आप कहाँ बैठेंगे?

'. (으)ㄹ게요 ' **I will do** (उल-केयो)

This is also a future tense verb ending like –을 거에요 but the difference is that this pattern **is only with first person**. This form is used for expressing the speaker's intention or plan or promise. It is used with action verbs as well as with the verb 있다 , but not with adjectives.

• 제가 할게요.	I will do it.
छेगा हाल्केयो.	इसे मैं करुंगा।
• 거기에서 기다릴게요.	I will wait over there.
खगीएसअ खिदारील्केयो.	मैं वहाँ इंतजार करुंगा।
• 내일 갈게요.	I will go tomorrow.
नेइल खाल्केयो.	मैं कल जाऊंगा।

• 제가 도와 드릴게요.	I will help you.
छेगा थोवा थुरील्केयो.	मैं आपकी मदद करुंगा।
• 저는 연락할게요.	I will contact you.
छनुन यल्लाक-हाल्केयो.	मैं आपसे संपर्क करुंगा।

3. Selected Patterns

a. '-고 있다 ':(someone) is doing (something) (गो इत्ता)

The pattern '-고 있다` is used to indicate a kind of process or continuing action. It is Present Continuous tense that shows that that action is going on/continued.

• 뭘 하고 있어요?	What are you doing now?
मुअल हागो इस्सअयो?	आप क्या कर रहे हैं?
• 한국어를공부 하고 있어요.	I'm studying Korean.
हांगुगअरुल खोम्बु हागो इस्सअयो.	मैं कोरियन पढ़ रहा हूँ।
• 친구를 기다리고 있어요.	I'm waiting for my friends.
छींगु-रुल खीदारिगो इस्सअयो.	मैं दोस्तों का इंतजार कर रहा हूँ।
• 선생님은 지금 식사하고 계세요.	Teacher is having meal now.
सन्सेंग-नीमुन छीगुम सीक्सा-हागो खेसेयो.	शिक्षक अभी भोजन कर रहे हैं।
• 엄마는 요리하고 있어요.	Mother is cooking food.
अम्मा-नुन योरी-हगो इस्सअयो.	माँ खाना बना रही है।

You can make the past and future tense sentences with the verb '있다 ' as following:-

• 친구를 기다리고 있었어요. छींगु-रुल खीदारिगो इस्सअयो.	I was waiting for my friends. मैं दोस्तों का इंतजार कर रहा था।
• 친구를 기다리고 있을 거예요. छींगु-रुल खीदारिगो इस्सुल-कयेयो.	I will be waiting for my friends. मैं दोस्तों का इंतजार करता रहूँगा।

There are two ways to make negative sentences with this pattern.

• 친구를 기다리고 있어요? छींगु-रुल खीदारिगो इस्सअयो?	Are you waiting for your friends? क्या तुम दोस्तों का इंतजार कर रहे हो?
• 아니오, 친구를 안 기다리고 있어요. आनिओ, छींगु-रुल आन खीदारिगो इस्सअयो.	No I'm not waiting for my friends. नहीं, दोस्तों का इंतजार नहीं कर रहा हूँ।
• 아니오, 친구를 기다리고 있지 않아요. आनिओ, छींगु-रुल खीदारिगो इच्ची आनायो.	No I'm not waiting for my friends. नहीं मैं दोस्तों का इंतजार नहीं कर रहा हूँ।

b. -고 싶다 ' : would like to (do)/want to (do) (गो शिप्ता)

The pattern '-고 싶다' is used to indicate the desire of the subject and is used with action verbs and '있다 .' This pattern '-고 싶다' is used with first person statements and second person questions. Remember that it is never used with descriptive verbs. Here are some examples:

• 사과를 사고 싶어요.	(I) would like to buy an apple.
साग्वारुल सागो शिफ़अयो.	मैं सेब खरीदना चाहता हूँ/चाहूँगा।
• 커피를 마시고 싶어요.	(I) would like to drink a cup of coffee.
खफीरुल माशीगो शिफ़अयो.	मैं कॉफी पीना चाहता हूँ/चाहूँगा।
• 한국에 가고 싶어요.	(I) would like to go to Korea.
हांगुगे खागो शिफ़अयो.	मैं कोरिया जाना चाहता हूँ/चाहूँगा।
• 안나씨를 만나고 싶어요?	Would (you) like to see Anna?
आन्ना शीरुल मान्नागो शिफ़अयो?	क्या आप मि. अन्ना से मिलना चाहते हैं/चाहेंगे?
• 저는 인도에 살고 싶어요.	I want to live in India.
छनुन इन्दो-ए साल्गो शिफ़अयो.	मैं भारत में रहना चाहता हूँ/चाहूँगा।

You can make the past and future tense sentences with the verb '싶다' as following:-

• 피자를 먹고 싶었어요.	(I) wanted to eat pizza.
फीजारुल मक्को शिफअ-स्सअयो.	मैं पिज़्ज़ा खाना चाहता हूँ/चाहूँगा।
• 피자를-먹고 싶지 않아요.	(I) don't want to eat pizza.
फीजारुल मक्को शिप्ची आनायो.	मैं पिज़्ज़ा खाना नहीं चाहता हूँ/चाहूँगा।

c. '-고 싶어하다':want to do –, would like to–(गो शिफअहादा)

As we studied, pattern '-고 싶다' is used only with first person statements and second person questions. The '-고 싶어하다' pattern is used to express desires in third person subject statements and questions with all verbs and '있다'.

• 라주씨가 어디에 가고 싶어 해요?	Where does Raju want to go?
राजू शीगा अदीए खागो शिफअ-हेयो.	राजू कहाँ जाना चाहता है?
• 라주씨는 집에 가고 싶어 해요.	Raju wants to go to home.
राजू शीनुन छीबे खागो शिफअ-हेयो.	राजू घर जाना चाहता है।
• 내하 씨가 무엇을 먹고 싶어 해요?	What does Neha want to eat?
नेहा शीगा मुअसल मक्को शिफअ-हेयो?	नेहा क्या खाना चाहती है?
• 내하 씨는 불고기를 먹고 싶어 해요.	Neha wants to eat Bulgogi.
नेहा शीनुन फुल्गोगीरुल मक्को शिफअ-हेयो.	नेहा फूलगोभी खाना चाहती है।

You can make the past and future tense sentences with the verb 가다 as following:-

• 미나씨가 어디에 가고 싶어 했어요?	Where did Mina want to go?
मीना शीगा अदीए खागो शिफल-हेस्सअयो?	मीना कहाँ जाना चाहती थी?
• 집에 가고 싶어 했어요	She wanted to go home.
छीबे खागो शिफअ-हेस्सअयो.	वह घर जाना चाहती थी।

Negation is expressed in the verb '싶어 하다' with '-지 않다', such as '싶어 하지 않아요'.

• 미나씨가 집에 가고 싶어 했어요?	Did Mina want to go home?
मीना-शीगा छीबे खागो शिफअ हे-स्सअयो?	क्या मीना घर जाना चाहती थी?
• 아니오, 집에 가고 싶어 하지 않았어요.	No, she didn't want to go home.
आनिओ, छीबे खागो शिफअ-हाजी अ:ना-स्सअयो.	नहीं, वह घर जाना नहीं चाहती थी।

d. '-세요':imperative Sentence ending (सेयो)

'-세요' is one of the sentence endings which can be used for indicating polite questioning in the Interrogative (-세요?) and polite order (command) in the Imperatives (-세요). Sometimes this pattern is also used for normal present tense statements instead of '-아요/어요.' This ending is more polite than the sentence ending '-아요/어요 .'

- **'-세요?' (सेयो?)**

The use of this form implies respect of the speaker for the subject of the sentence. But if someone asks you a question using this pattern, the answer to this '-세요?' must be in plain form '-아요/어요 ' that means you must refer to yourself with respect.

Ex:

• 집에 가세요?	Do you go home?
छीबे खासेयो?	क्या आप घर जा रहे हैं?

• 네, 집에 가요.	Yes, I go.
ने, छीबे खायो.	हाँ घर जा रहा हूँ।
• 선생님, 요즘 어떻게 지내세요?	Sir, how have you been lately?
सन्सेंग-नीम, योजुम अत्तअखे छीने-सेयो?	सर, आप कैसे हैं?
• 잘 지내요.	I have been fine.
छाल छीनेयो.	मैं बिल्कुल ठीक हूँ।
박 씨는매일 운동을 하세요.	Mr. Park does exercise every-day.
फाक-सीनुन मेइल उन्दोंगुल हासेयो.	मि. पार्क प्रतिदिन व्यायाम करते है।

• **'-세요?' (सेयो?)**

This form also means 'Please do something' when referring to the second person.

• 사과 주세요.	Please give me an apple.
साग्वा छूसेयो	सेब दीजिए।
• 미나를 만나세요.	Please meet Meena.
मीनारुल मान्नासेयो.	मीना से मिल लीजिए।
• 여기 앉으세요.	Please sit here.
यगी आन्जु-सेयो.	यहाँ बैठिए।
• 열심히 공부하세요.	Please study well.
यल-सीम्ही खोम्बु-हासेयो.	मेहनत से पढ़ाई कीजिए।

- 이 일을 빨리 하세요. Please do this work soon.
  इ इरुल पाल्ली हासेयो. इस काम को जल्दी कीजिए।

---

e. '-(으)십시오 ' the imperative form (शिप्सीयो)

This is also an imperative verb form but it is more polite than '-세요' pattern. Sentences are made by attaching '-(으)십시오.' to the verb stem. '-십시오' is used after verb stems ending in a vowel and '으십시오' after verb stems ending with a consonant

Ex.:

오다 : 오 + 십시오 오십시오.

입다 : 입 + 으십시오. 입으십시오.

- 어서 오십시오. Please come in.
  असअ .ओशीप्सीओ. कृपया अन्दर आइए।
- 다음 장을 읽으십시오. Please read the next chapter.
  थाउम जांगुल इल्गअ-शीप्सीओ. कृपया अगले अध्याय को पढ़िए।
- 여기 이름을 쓰십시오. Please write your name here.
  यगी इरुमुल सुशीप्सीओ. कृपया यहाँ अपना नाम लिखिए।
- 잠깐만 기다리십시오. Please wait here.
  छाम्कान-मान खीदारी-शीप्सीओ. कृपया यहाँ थोड़ा इंतजार कीजिए।
- 잘 들으십시오. Please listen carefully.
  छाल थुरअशीप्सीओ. कृपया ध्यान से सुनिए।

---

f. ' -(으)ㄹ까요?' Shall we (I) ~ ?/Will it be ~ ? (उल्कायो)

The pattern '-(으)ㄹ까요?' is used to express

proposal or inquiring about someone's opinion, view or appraisal on a certain matter or fact with the action verb.

In this case, the subject of the sentence will always be the first person, singular or plural i.e. I or We.

• 우리 거기에서 **만날까요?**	Shall we meet there?
ऊरी खगीएसअ मन्नाल्कायो?	क्या हम वहाँ मिलें?
• 무엇을 **할까요?**	What shall I do?
मुअसल हाल्कायो?	मैं क्या करूँ?
• 늦었으니까 비행기로 **갈까요?**	Because we are late, shall we go by airplane?
नजअसअ-नीका फीहेंगीरो खाल्कायो?	चूँकि देर हो गई है, क्या हम हवाई-जहाज से चलें?
• 오늘 저녁에 모한 집에 갈까요?	Shall we go to Mohan's home today evening?
ओनुल छन्यगे मोहन छीबे खाल्कायो?	क्या आज शाम मोहन के घर चलें?
• 차를 한잔 할까요?	Shall we take a cup of tea?
छारुल हान्जान-हाल्कायो?	क्या एक कप चाय पियें?

g. '-(으)ㅂ시다': let's —(propositive) (उप्शीदा)

This form is used to expressing the subject's suggestion with the action verbs and the verb of existence '있다'. If someone asks a question using '-(으)ㄹ까요' generally the answer is given with '- 읍시다' pattern.

Ex:

• 내일 영화를 보러 갈까요? नेइल यन्गह्वा-रुल फोरअ खाल्कायो?	Shall we go for a movie? क्या कल फिल्म देखने चलें?
• 네, 갑시다. ने, खप्सीदा.	Yes, let's go. हाँ, चलतें हैं।

'-읍시다.' is used after verb stems ending in a consonant.

먹(다) + -읍시다 → 먹읍시다.

'-ㅂ시다' is used after verb stems ending in a vowel.

가(다) + -ㅂ 시다 → 갑시다.

• **빨리 갑시다.** पाल्ली खाप्सीदा.	Let's go quickly. चलो, जल्दी चलते हैं।
• 한국어를 공부**합시다.** हांगगरुल खोम्बु-हाप्सीदा.	Let's study Korean. चलो, कोरियन पढ़ते हैं।
• 여기에 **앉읍시다.** यगीए आन्जअप्सीदा.	Let's sit here. चलो, यहाँ बैठते हैं।
• 기차로 **갑시다.** खीच्छारो खाप्सीदा.	Let's go by train. चलो, ट्रेन से चलते हैं।
• 이번 주말에 만**납시다.** इबन छूमारे मान्नाप्सीदा.	Let's meet this weekend. इस साप्ताहान्त पर मिलते हैं।

Remember that it cannot be used with '이다' nor with descriptive verbs.

h. '-(으)면 ':'if, when ...' (म्यन)

The connective '-(으) 면 ' can be used with any verb or adjective and indicates condition. While in English a dependent clause which is introduced with 'if' can either precede or follow the main clause, in Korean the dependent clause precedes the main clause. It simply means that condition will always come before the main clause.

'-면' is used when verb stem ends with a vowel and '-으면' is used when verb stem ends with a consonant except '-ㄹ'.

• 그 영화가 재미있**으면** 보겠어요. ख यंगह्वागा छेमी-इस्सअम्यन फोगेस्सअयो.	If the movie is interesting, I will see it. अगर यह फिल्म रोचक हुई तो मैं इसे देखूंगा।
• 비가 오**면** 가지 마세요. फीगा ओम्यन खाजी मासेयो.	If it rains, please don't go. अगर बारिश होती है, तो मत जाइऐ।
• 시간이 있으면 우리 집에 오세요. शिगानी इस्सअम्यन उरी छेबे ओसेया.	If you have time, please come to my house. अगर समय हो, तो हमारे घर आइए।
• 델리에 오시면 연락해 주세요. थेल्ली-ए ओसी-म्यन यल्लाक-हे छूसेयो.	If you come to Delhi, please contact me. अगर आप दिल्ली आएँ मुझसे संपर्क करें।
• 이 책을 좋아하면 가지 세요. इ छेगुल छोआ-हाम्यन खाजीसेयो.	If you like this book, take it. अगर यह किताब आपको अच्छी लगती है तो इसे ले जाइए।

i. 에 (ऐ)

It's a locative particle. It's used after place shows that something exists there or movement to that place.

Remember that it will not be used after place when some action is going on there (In that case we use 에서). It is also used to denote time or direction. It is similar to 'in/at or to.'

• 가족이 한국에 있어요. (Location)	My family is in Korea.
खाजोगी हांगुगे इस्सअयो.	मेरा परिवार कोरिया में है।
• 밤에 책을 읽어요. (Time)	I read a book at night.
फामे छेगुल इल्गयो.	मैं रात में किताब पढ़ता हूँ।
• 지금 은행에 가요. (Direction)	I go to the bank now.
छीगुम उन्हेंगे खायो.	मैं अभी बैंक जा रहा हूँ।
• 한시에 만날까요? (Time)	Shall we meet at 1 o'clock?
हान सीए मान्नाल-कायो?	क्या हम 1 बजे मिलें?
• 타즈마할은아그라에 있어요. (Location)	Tajmahal is in Agra.
ताज महरन आगरा-ए इस्सअयो.	ताजमहल आगरा में है।

j. - 에서 (एसअ)

It's a particle having two meanings: 'in/at' and 'from.' When it means 'in/at' there must be an action taking place. When the sentence shows any movement, 에서 means 'from.'

• 경준 씨는 한국에서 왔어요. (from)	Mr. khyung Jun has come from Korea.

ख्यंग जुन शीनुन हांगुगेसअ वा-स्सअयो.	मि. ख्यंग जून कोरिया से आए हैं।
• 극장에서 영화를 봅니다. (in/at)	I see movie at the theatre.
खक्चांगेसअ यंग-ह्वा-रुल फोम्नीदा.	मैं थियेटर में फिल्म देखता हूँ।
• 제 집에서 시장까지 멀어요.	It's far from my house to market.
छे छीबेसअ सीजांग-काजी मरअयो.	मेरे घर से बाजार दूर है।
• 그는 도서관에서 공부하고 있어요.	He is studying in the library.
खुनुन थोसअ-ग्वान-एसअ खोम्बुहागो इस्सअयो.	वह पुस्तकालय में पढ़ रहा है।
• 이 옷을 남대문 시장에서 샀어요.	I brought this cloth from Nam-demun market.
इ ओसुल नाम्देमुन सीजांग-एसअ सास्सअयो.	मैंने यह कपड़ा नाम्देमुन बाजार से खरीदा।

k. 와/과 (वा/ग्वा)

This particle links two nouns and has the meaning of 'and/together.' 와 is used when the noun ends in a vowel and 과 is used when the noun ends in a consonant.

• 치마와 바지를 샀어요. (noun ends in a vowel)	I bought a skirt and trousers.
छीमावा फाजीरुल सास्सअयो.	मैंने स्कर्ट और पैंट खरीदी।
• 밥과 반찬을 먹어요.	I eat rice and side dishes
फाप-क्वा फान्छानुल मगअयो.	मैंने चावल और अन्य चीजें खायीं।
• 선생님과 학생들이	Teacher and students are in

• 교실에 있어요.	the classroom.
सन्सेंग-नीम-ग्वा हाक्सेंग-दुरी ख्योसीरे इस्सअयो.	शिक्षक और छात्र कक्षा में हैं।
• 람씨는 한국어와 일본어·어를 공부해요.	Ram studies Korean and Japanese.
राम-सीनुन हांगुगअ-वा इल्बोन-अरुल खोम्बु-हेयो.	मि. राम कोरियन और जापानी भाषाए पढ़ते हैं।
• 철수와미라는 다음 달에인도에 갈 거에요.	Chulsoo and Meera will go to India next month.
छल्सू-वा मीरा-नुन धाउम दारे इन्दोए खाल-कएयो.	छल्सू और मारिश अगले महीने अमेरिका जाएंगे।

1. 에게/께 (एगे/के)

에게 means 'to' and is used with persons or animals and not with the place.

• 친구에게 편지를 보냈어요.	I sent a letter to my friend.
छींगु-एगे फ्यन्जी-रुल फोने-स्सअयो.	मैंने दोस्त को पत्र भेजा।
• 동생에게 과자를 주었어요	I gave cookies to my brother.
थोंग्सें-एगे ख्वाजारुल छुअ-स्सअयो.	(मैंने) छोटे भाई को बिस्कुट दिया।
• 여자 친구에게 선물을 주었어요.	I gave gift to my girlfriend.
यजा-छींगु-एगे सन्मुरुल छुअ-स्सअयो.	मैंने अपनी गर्लफ्रेंड को उपहार दिया।

–께 is the honorific form of-에게. It is used with elders or respectable persons.

• 선생님께 전화를 걸었어요	I called my teacher.
सन्सेंग-नीम-के छन्हा-रुल खरअ-स्सअयो.	शिक्षक महोदय को फोन किया।
• 어머니께 꽃을 드렸어요.	I gave flowers to mother.
अमनी-के कोछुल थुर्यअ-स्सअयो.	माँ को फूल दिए।

m. - 에서~~~ 까지/ 부터~~~ 까지 (एसेअ.....काजी/बुथअ.... काजी)

-에서 (and -부터) means 'from' and -까지 means 'to/till.' They are attached to nouns and show the starting/finishing place or points of time of the action. -에서~~~ -까지 is used with place while -부터~~~ -까지 is used with time and with place also.

- 여기부터 델리 대학교까지 얼마나 걸려요?
  यगी-बुथअ थेल्ली देहाक्यो-काजी अल्माना खल्ययो?
  How long does it take from here to Delhi University?
  यहाँ से दिल्ली विश्वविद्यालय कितनी दूर है।
- 인도에서 한국까지 여덟 시간 걸려요. (Place)
  इन्दो-एसअ हांगुक-काजी यदल शीगान खल्ययो?
  It takes 8 hours from India to Korea.
  भारत से कोरिया तक आठ घंटे लगते हैं।
- 월요일부터 금요일까지 학교에 갑니다.(Time)
  वर्योइल-बुथअ खुम्योइल-काजी हाक्योए खायों.
  I go to school from Monday to Friday.

मैं सोमवार से शुक्रवार तक विद्यालय जाता हूँ।

- 아침 6 시부터 7 까지 운동을 해요.

  आछीम यसत-सी-बुथअ इल्गोप-सी-काजी उन्दोंगुल हेयो.

  I do exercise in the morning from 6 o'clock to 7 o'clock.

  मैं सुबह 6 बजे से 7 बजे तक व्यायाम करता हूँ।

- 우리 호텔에서 사로지니 나가르 마켓이 가까워요

  उरी होथेरसअ सरोजिनी नगर माखेशी खाक्का-वयो.

  Sarojini Nagar market is near from our hotel.

  सरोजिनी नगर मार्केट हमारे होटल से नजदीक है।

n. (으)로 **(उरो) की ओर/से**

There are two usage of this particle. It can be used both as a directive particle or instrumental particle. When used in the sense of movement, it shows direction, similar to 'to/towards.' But when used as an instrumental particle, it means method, medium or tool, similar to 'by, with.'

-로 is used when the noun stem ends in a vowel or consonant ㄹ. 으로 is used when the noun stem ends in a consonant.

- 저는 기숙사로 갑니다. — I am going to hostel.

  छनुन खीसुक्सा-रो खायो. — मैं छात्रावास की ओर जा रहा हूँ।

- 시장으로 갑시다. — Let's go to market.

  शीजांग-अरो खाप्सीदा. — चलो, बाजार की ओर चलते हैं।

- 그는 버스로 왔어요. — He came by bus.

खुनुन बसुरो वास्सअयो.	वह बस से आया।
• 한국말로 말합시다.	Let's speak in Korean.
हांगुंग-माल्लो मार-हाप्सीदा.	चलो, कोरियन में बोलते हैं।
• 시험지에 연필로 쓰세요.	Write with pencil in the exam paper.
सीहम-जीए यन्फील्लो ससेयो.	परीक्षा पुस्तिका में पेन्सिल से लिखें।

o.' 안 ':Not (आन) —'नहीं'

The adverb '안 ' is used to express the negative and means 'do not'. '안 ' is put before the verb. It can be used with any tense or pattern.

• 나는어제 학교에 안 갔어.	I did not go to school.
अजे हाक्योए आन खास्सअयो.	मैं कल स्कूल नहीं गया।
• 점심을 안 먹었어요.	He didn't take lunch.
छम्सीमुल आन मगअ-स्सअयो.	उसने भोजन नहीं किया।
• 어제 친구를 안 만났어요.	Yesterday I didn't meet my friend.
अजे छींगु-रुल आन मान्ना-स्सअयो.	कल मैं अपने मित्र से नहीं मिला।
• 오늘은 누가 안 왔어요?	Who hasn't come today?
ओनरुन नुगा आन वास्सअयो?	आज कौन नहीं आया है।
• 인도 사람들이 왜 고기를 잘 안 먹어요?	Why do Indians not eat ?
इन्दो-साराम-दुरी वे खोंगीरुल छाल आन मगअयो?	भारतीय मांस क्यों नहीं खाते हैं?

p. '못 ':want to do but can not (मोत)–नहीं कर सकना

The adverb '못 ' is used with action verbs, and means impossibility or strong denial and refusal.

• 파티에 못 갔어요. फाथीए मोत खा-स्सअयो.	I could not go to party. मैं पार्टी में नहीं गया।
• 형을 못 만났어요. ह्यंगुल मोत् मान्ना-स्सअयो.	I could not meet my elder brother. मैं अपने बड़े भाई से नहीं मिल सका।
• 오늘은 학교에 못 가요. ओनरुन हाक्योए मोत खायो.	I can not go to school today. आज मैं स्कूल नहीं जा सकता हूँ।
• 점심을 못 먹었어요. छम्सीमुल मोत मग-स्सअयो.	I could not take lunch. मैं लंच नहीं कर पाया।
• 내일 친구를 못 만나겠어요. नेइरुन छींगु-रुल मोत मान्ना-गेस्सअयो.	Tomorrow I would not be able to meet my friend. कल मैं अपने मित्र से नहीं मिल पाऊँगा।

q. '옆/ 앞 / 뒤 / 위 / 아래 + 에' : beside/in fromt of/behind/on/under (यफ/आफ/थ्वी/वी/आरे+ए) बगल में/सामने/पीछे/ऊपर/नीचे

These are the words that indicate directions and locations. Combined with markers indicating location such as '에 `, they are used for locations.

• 고양이가 책상 옆에 있어요. खोयांगीगा छेक्सांग-यफे इस्सअयो.	There is a cat beside the desk.
• 의자가책상 앞에 있어요.	There is a chair in front of the desk.

खोयांगीगा छेक्सांग-आफे इस्सअयो.

- 창문이 책상 뒤에 있어요. — There is a window behind the desk.

  खोयांगीगा छेक्सांग-थ्वीए इस्सअयो.
- 책이 책상 위에 있어요. — There is a book on the desk.

  खोयांगीगा छेक्सांग-वीए इस्सअयो.
- 구두가 책상 아래에 있어요. — Shoes are under the desk.

  खोयांगीगा छेक्सांग-आरेए इस्सअयो.

---

r. -보다 ':(more) than (फोदा) –से (अधिक)

The comparative marker '보다 ' (more than) is attached to a standard of comparison (which is usually the second noun) when both items of comparison are mentioned. It is often accompanied by '-더 ' which means 'more' but the use of '-더 ' is optional.

• 한국말이 영어보다 (더). 어려워요.	Korean is more difficult than English.
हांगुंग-मारी यंगअ-फोदा (थअ) अर्यअ-वयो.	कोरियन अंग्रेंजी से ज्यादा कठिन है।
• 개가 고양이보다 (더) 커요.	Dogs are bigger than cats.
खेगा खोयांगी-फोदा (थअ) खयो.	कुत्ता बिल्ली से बड़ा होता है।
• 오늘은 어제보다 (더) 시원해요.	Today is cooler than yesterday.
ओनुरुन अजे-फोदा (थअ) शीवनहेयो	आज मौसम कल से ठंडा है।

When the standard of comparison is omitted, '더 ' ('more) is used.

• 이것은더 좋아요.	This is better.
इगअसन थअ छोआयो.	यह ज्यादा अच्छा है।
• 한국말이 더 어려워요.	Korean is more difficult.
हांगुंग-मारी थअ अर्यअ-वयो.	कोरियन ज्यादा कठिन है।
• 나는 사과가 더 좋아요.	I like apples more.
नानुन साग्वागा थअ छोआयो.	मुझे सेब ज्यादा अच्छा लगता है।

s. '-지만 ':but (जीमान)–'लेकिन'

This connective is used to join two sentences which are in contrast with each other.

• 바쁘지만, 도와드리겠어요.	I'm busy, but I will help you.
फापुजीमान, थोवा थुरी-गेस्सअयो.	मैं व्यस्त हूँ लेकिन आपकी मदद करुँगा।
• 열심히 공부했지만, 아직 잘 못해요.	I studied hard, but I am not able do well yet.
यल्शीम्ही खोम्बु-हेच्चीमान, आजीक छाल मोत्थेयो.	मैंने कड़ी मेहनत की पर अभी भी इसे ठीक से नहीं समझ पाया हूँ।
• 가고 싶었지만, 가지 않았어요.	I wanted to go, but I didn't.
छनन खागो शीफअ-चीमान, खाजी मोत-हे-स्सअयो.	मैं जाना चाहता था पर नहीं गया।
• 이 책이 좋지만 비싸요.	This book is good but expensive.
इ छेगी छोछीमान फीस्सायो.	यह किताब अच्छी है पर मंहगी है।

t. 그리고 (खुरीगो) और

It links two sentences on equal basis or shows order, similar to 'and.'

• 선물을 샀어요. 그리고 친구에게 줬어요. सन्मुरुल सास्सअयो. खुरीगो छींगु-एगे छुव-स्सअयो.	I bought a gift and gave it to my friend. मैंने उपहार खरीदा और दोस्त को दिया।
• 이 식당이 좋아요. 그리고 싸요. इ सीक्तांगी छोआयो. खुरीगो सायो.	This restaurant is good and cheap. यह रेस्टोरेंट अच्छा और सस्ता है।
• 어제 책을 읽었어요. 그리고 잤어요. अजे छेगुल इल्गअस्सअयो. खुरीगो छास्सअयो.	Yesterday, I read a book. And (then) I slept. कल मैंने एक किताब पढ़ी और फिर सो गया।
• 한 시에 학교에서 돌아왔어요. 그리고 점심을 먹었어요. हान सी-ए हाक्यो-एसअ थोरा-वास्सअयो. खुरीगो छम्सीमुल मगअ-स्सअयो.	I returned from school at 1 o'clock. Then I took lunch. मैं स्कूल से 1 बजे लौटा। फिर मैंने लंच किया।

u. 그러나/ 그렇지만 (खुरना/खुरअछीमान) लेकिन

They are used when content of two sentences are opposite or contrasting, similar to 'but/however.'

- 가고 싶었어요. 그러나 가지 않았어요.
  I wanted to go. But I didn't.
  छनन खागो शीफअ-स्सअयो. खुरअना खाजी आना-स्सअयो.
  मैं जाना चाहता था पर नहीं गया।
- 옷이 비싸요. 그러나/ 그렇지만 예뻐요.
  The cloth is expensive but beautiful.
  ओशी फीस्सायो. खुरना/खुरअछीमान येप्पयो.
  कपड़ा मंहगा है पर सुन्दर है।
- 일요일입니다. 그러나/ 그렇지만 일찍 일어났어요.
  It is Sunday, but I got up early.
  इर्यो-इरीम्नीदा. खुरना/खुरअछीमान इल्चीक इरअ-नास्सअयो.

आज रविवार है पर मैं जल्दी जाग गया।

- 외국어 공부는 어려워요. 그러나/ 그렇지만 재미있어요.
  Foreign language study is difficult but it's interesting.
  वेगुगअ खोम्बू-नन अर्यअवयो. खुरना/खुरअछीमान छेमी-इस्सअयो.
  कोरिया पढ़ना कठिन है पर रोचक है।
- 저는 글씨를 써요. 그러나/ 그렇지만 못 읽어요.
  I can write alphabets but I cannot read.
  छनुन खुल्सी-रुल सयो. खुरना/खुरअछीमान मोत इल्गअयो.
  मैं अक्षर लिख लेता हूँ पर पढ़ नहीं सकता हूँ।
- 바나나는 맛있어요. 그러나/ 그렇지만 저는 안 좋아해요.
  Banana is delicious. But I don't like it
  बनाना-नन मासी-स्सअयो. खरुना/खरअछीमान, छनुन आन छोहा-हेयो।
  केला स्वादिष्ट है पर मुझे पसंद नहीं है।

v. 그러면/ 그럼 (खुरम/खुरअम्यन) 'तो, तब'

They are used like 'then, if so, in that case.' The first sentence is generally a presumption of the second sentence.

- 시간이 늦었습니다. It's late.
  शीगानी नुजस्सुम्नीदा. देर हो गयी है।
- 그럼/그러면 택시를 탑시다. Then let's take a taxi.
  खुरम/खुरअम्यन थेक्सीरुल थाप्सीदा. तब टैक्सी से चलते है।
- 너무 덥습니다. It's very hot.
  नमू थप्सुम्नीदा. बहुत गर्मी है।
- 그럼/그러면 샤워를 하세요. Then take a shower.
  खुरम/खुरअम्यन शावअरुल हासेयो. तब नहा लीजिए।
- 선생님! 질문이 있어요. Teacher/Sir! I have a question.
  सन्सेंग-नीम! छील्मुनी इस्सअयो. महाशय, मेरे पास एक प्रश्न है।

• 그럼/그러면 물어 보세요.	Then ask it.
खुरम/खुरअम्यन मुरअ बोसेयो.	तब पूछो/पूछिए।
• 일요일에 시간이 없어요	I don't have time on Sunday.
इर्योइरे शीगानी अप्सअयो.	रविवार को मेरे पास समय नहीं है।
• 그럼/그러면 월요일에 갑시다.	Then, let's go on Monday.
खुरम/खुरअम्यन वर्योइरे खाप्सीदा.	तब सोमवार को चलते हैं।

W. 그래서 (खुरेसअ) 'इसलिए'

This connecter is equivalent to 'so.' The first sentence becomes the cause of or reason for the next sentence.

• 늦었습니다. 그래서 택시를 탔어요.	We were late. So we took a taxi.
नुजअ-स्सुम्नीदा. खुरेसअ थेक्सीरुल थास्सअयो.	देर हो गयी थी, इसीलिए हमने टैक्सी ले ली।
• 출근 시간입니다. 그래서 교통이 복잡해요.	It's office hour. So traffic is heavy.
छुल्गुन शीगा-नीम्नीदा. खुरेसअ ख्योथोंगी फोक्चाफेयो.	यह ऑफिस का समय है, इसीलिए यातायात बहुत व्यस्त है।
• 공부를 많이 해요. 그래서 성적이 좋아요.	I study a lot. So my grades are good.
खोम्बु-रुल मानी हेयो. खुरेसअ संग्जगी छोआयो.	मैं बहुत पढ़ाई करता हूँ, इसीलिए मेरे ग्रेड अच्छे हैं।
• 이 나무는 커요. 그래서 좋아요.	This tree is big. So I like it.
इ नामुनन खयो. खुरेसअ छोआयो.	यह पेड़ बड़ा है, इसीलिए मुझे पसंद है।

- 저는 과학을 좋아해요. 그래서 대학교에 갔어요. — I like science. So I went to college.
  छनुन ख्वाहागुल छोआहेयो. खुरेसअ देहाक्योए खास्सअयो. — मुझे विज्ञान पसंद है, इसीलिए मैं कॉलेज गया।

---

5. HONORIFIC SYSTEM

Korean has two types of honorifics.

a. One type is expressed by combining '-시- ' with verbs, indicating respect on the part of the speaker for the listner. The honorific form is made by inserting '-(으)시-' between the verb stem and the endings like -아(어/여)요, '었어요, -ㅂ니다, 었어요, -ㅂ니다, 었습니다, -ㅂ니까? or 었습니까? '-시- is used when verb stem ends in a vowel and '-으시- ' is used when verb stem ends in a consonant.

가다	가 + 시 + 어요	가 + 시어요	가세요
받다	받 + 으시 + 어요	받 + 으시어요	받으세요
오다	오 + 시 + 었어요	오 + 시었어요	오셨어요
읽다	읽 + 으시 + 었어요	읽 + 으시었어요	읽으셨어요.
하다	하 + 시 + ㅂ니다	하십니다	하십니다
찾다	찾 + 으시 + 었어요	찾 + 으시었어요	찾으셨어요.

b. The other way is to use respective forms of verb. They are special and seperate honorific words used by the speaker to express his/her own humility and, simultaneously, show his/her respect for the person with whom he is speaking. These honorifics are used when the person deserving respect is the object of the sentence.

Plain Form	Honorific Form	Meaning
주다	드리다	to give
묻다(말하다)	여쭈다/여쭙다 말씀하시다	to ask/to tell
보다	뵙다	to see/to meet
데리고 가다/오다	모시고 가다/ 오다	to take /bring someone to somewhere
먹다	잡수시다	to eat
자다	주무시다	to sleep
있다	계시다	to exist, to be
아프다	편찮다	to be sick

• 많이 잡수세요. मानी छाप्सुसेयो.	Help yourself. खूब खाइए।
• 김선생님 계세요? किम सन्सेंग-नीम खेसेयो?	Is Mr. Kim there? क्या मि. किम हैं?
• 어머님께서 많이 편찮으세요? अमनीम-केसअ मानी फ्यन्छा-नसेयो?	Is your mother seriously sick? क्या आपकी माताजी बहुत बीमार हैं?
• 잘 주무세요. छाल छुमुसेयो.	Good Night. शुभ रात्रि।
• 오늘 선생님을 뵙겠어요. ओनुल सन्सेंग-नीमुल फ्वेप-केस्सअयो.	I will meet my teacher today. आज मैं अपने शिक्षक से मिलूँगा।

6. NUMBER SYSTEM

Pure Korean and Sino-korean words

Two sets of numbers are used in Korean: native Korean and Sino-Korean. Sino-Korean numbers are the words that are borrowed from Chinese language.

Here are the both sets of couting number (1 to 10).

Pure Korean numbers		Sino-Korean numbers	
1 하나	हाना	일	इल
2 둘	थुल	이	ई
3 셋	सेत	삼	साम
4 넷	नेत	사	सा
5 다섯	थासत	오	ओ
6 여섯	यसत	육	युक
7 일곱	इल्गोप	칠	छील
8 여덟	यदल	팔	फाल
9 아홉	आहोप	구	खु
10 열	यल	십	शीप

There is no semantic difference between the two sets. Both '하나' and '일 ' means 'one'. They differ according to their usage in different contexts. For example, Sino Korean counting system is used while counting the (small) numbers of person, age, money,year, minutes, whereas pure Korean numbers are used for counting the following

- Months
- Days
- Minutes
- Currency
- Phone numbers

First, let us learn more about the Chinese numbers. Counting more than ten observes the arithmetic principles. Take "12" and "20" for example. 12 is made of 10 and 2. On the other hand, 20 stands for two tens. Thus, the Chinese number has them:

12 = 10 + 2 십 이

20 = 2 x 10 이 십

Sino-korean numbers under 100

10	11	12	13	14
십	십일	십이	십삼	십사
शीप	**शीप इल**	**शीप ई (शीबी)**	**शीप शाम**	**शीप सा**
15	16	17	18	19
십오	십육	십칠	십팔	십구
शीप ओ	**शीप युक्**	**शीप छील**	**शीप फाल**	**शीप खु**
20	21	22	23	24
이십	이십일	이십이	이십삼	이십사
ई शीप	**ई शीप इल**	**ई शील ई**	**ई शीप साम**	**ई शीप सा**
25	26	27	28	29
이십오	이십육	이십칠	이십팔	이십구
ई शीप ओ	**ई शीप युक्**	**ई शीप छील**	**ई शीप फाल**	**ई शीप खु**

Tens, hundreds, thousands

0	1	2	3	4	5
영	일	이	삼	사	오
यंग	इल	ई	साम	सा	ओ
Tens	10	20	30	40	50
십	십	이십	삼십	사십	오십
शीप	शीप	ई शीप	साम शीप	सा शीप	ओ शीप
Hundreds	100	200	300	400	500
백	백	이백	삼백	사백	오백
बैंक	बैक	ई बैक	साम बैक	सा बैक	ओ बैक
Thousands	1,000	2,000	3,000	4,000	5,000
천	천	이천	삼천	사천	오천
छन	छन	ई छन	साम छन	सा छन	ओ छन
10 thousand.	10,000	20,000	30,000	40,000	50,000
만	만	이만	삼만	사만	오만
मान	मान	ई मान	साम मान	सा मान	ओ मान

♦ ♦ ♦

Section-IV
Useful Vocabulary

Word Glossary

Verbs

English	Hangeul	Pronunciation
To beat	두드리다	थुदुरीदा
To bend	구부리다	खुबुरीदा
To bind	묶다	मुक्ता
To boil	끓이다	करीदा
To break	꺾다	कक्ता
To break	부수다	फुशुदा
To bumped Into	부딪히다	फुदीछीदा
To burn	태우다	थेउदा
To bury	묻다	मुत्ता
To call	부르다	फुरुदा
To catch	잡다	छाप्ता
To change	바꾸다	फाक्कुदा

To chew	씹다	सीप्ता
To chop	조각내다	छोगांग्नेदा
To collapse	무너지다	मुनअ जीदा
To comb	빗다	फीत्ता
To come	오다	ओदा
To cool	식히다	शीखीदा
To cover	덮다	थप्ता
To cry	울다	उल्दा
To cut	끊다	कन्था
To dance	(춤)추다	छुम छुदा
To dig	파다	फादा
To drink	마시다	माशीदा
To drive	몰다(운전하다)	मोल्दा (उन्जन हादा)
To drop	떨어뜨리다	तरअ-तरीदा
To eat	먹다	मक्ता
To erase	지우다	छीउदा
To fall	넘어지다	नमअ-जीदा
To fix	고치다	खोछींदा
To fold	접다	छप्ता
To frown	찡그리다	चीन्गुरीदा
To fry	튀기다	थ्वीगीदा
To give	주다	छुदा
To go	가다	खादा
To grind	갈다	खाल्दा
To hang	매달다	मेदाल्दा
To hang	걸다	खल्दा

To have	갖다	खात्ता
To hear	듣다	थुत्ता
To heat	달구다	थाल्गुदा
To hold	끼다	कीदा
To hold	쥐다	छवीदा
To hold Up	들어 올리다	थुरअ-ओल्लीदा
To holler	외치다	वेछीदा
To improve	증진하다	छुंगजीन-हादा
To kick	차다	छादा
To kaugh	웃다	उत्ता
To learn	배우다	फ़ेउदा
To lie down	눕다	नुप्ता
To lock	잠그다	छाम्गुदा
To lose	잃다	इल्था
To make	만들다	मान्दुल्दा
To make	시키다	शीखीदा
To measure	재다	छेदा
To melt	녹이다	नोगीदा
To miss	놓치다	नोछीदा
To mix	섞다	सक्ता
To øpen	열다	यल्दा
To open	펼치다	फ्यल्छीदा
To parch	볶다	फोक्ता
To paste	바르다	फारुदा
To pay	지불하다	छीबुल हादा

To photograph	사진찍다	साजीन चीक्ता
To pick	쑤시다	सुशीदा
To pick up	집다	छीप्ता
To pile up	쌓다	सात्था
To play	놀다	नोल्दा
To polish	닦다	थाक्ता
To pour	따르다	तारुदा
To press	누르다	नूरूदा
To protect	감싸다	खाम्सादा
To pull	당기다	थांगीदा
To pull	끌다	कुल्दा
To pull out	꺼내다	कनेदा
To push	밀다	मिल्दा
To put	놓다	नोत्था
To put between	끼우다	कीउदा
To put down	내리다	नेरीदा
To put in	넣다	नत्था
To put off	(옷) 벗다	(ओत) फ़त्ता
To put on	얹다	अन्ता
To put on	(옷) 입다	(ओत) इप्ता
To put on	(신발) 신다	(शिन्बाल) शिन्दा
To put on	차다	छादा
To put on	붙이다	फुच्छीदा

To raise	올리다	ओल्लीदा
To read	읽다	इक्ता
To repair	고치다	खोच्छीदा
To rinse away	헹구다	हेंगुदा
To roast	굽다	खुप्ता
To roll	말다	माल्दा
To rub	문지르다	मुन्जीरुदा
To run	달리다	थाल्लीदा
To rush	서두르다	सथुरुदा
To scratch	긁다	खक्ता
To search	찾다	छात्ता
To see	보다	फोदा
To shout	소리치다	सोरीछीदा
To shut	닫다	थात्ता
To shut Up	다물다	थामुल्दा
To sit	앉다	आन्ता
To sleep	자다	छादा
To smoke	피우다	फीउदा
To soak	담그다	थाम्गुदा
To spread	펴다	फ्यदा
To sprinkle	뿌리다	पुरीदा
To stained	묻다	मुत्ता

To stamp	(도장)찍다	(थोजान्गा) चीक्ता
To stand up	일어나다	इरअ-नादा
To stand up	서다	सदा
To stir	젓다	छत्ता
To stop	멈추다	मम्छुदा
To strike	치다	छीदा
To strike	때리다	तेरीदा
To struck	맞다	मात्ता
To suck	빨다	पाल्दा
To take	타다	थादा
To take	받다	फात्ता
To take off	내리다	नेरीदा
To take off	떼다	तेदा
To take out	빼다	पेदा
To talk	말하다	मारहादा
To tear	찢다	चीत्ता
To hrow	던지다	थन्जीदा
To throw away	버리다	बरीदा
To turn	넘기다	नम्गीदा
To turn off	끄다	कुदा
To turn over	뒤집다	थ्विजिप्ता
To undo	원상태로 돌리다	वन्सांगथेरो थोल्लीदा

To wake up	깨다	केदा
To walk	걷다	खत्ता
To wash	씻다	सित्ता
To write	쓰다	सुदा
To write	적다	छक्ता

Weather

English	Hangeul	Pronunciation
Chilly	싸늘한	सानुल्हान
Cold	추운	छुउन
Cold	차가운	छागाउन
Cool	시원한	शीवन–हान
Cool	선선한	सनसनहान
Dry	건조한	खनजोहान
Hot	더운	थऊन
Humid	습한	सुफान
Rainy	비가 내리는	फीगा नेरीनन
Rough	거친	खछीन
Scorching	몹시 뜨거운	मेपसी तुगअउन
Shiny	빛나는	फीन्नानन
Snowy	눈이 내리는	नूनी नेरीनन
Warm	따뜻한	तात्तथान
Windy	바람이 부는	फारामी फूनन

Emotions

English	Hangeul	Pronunciation
Admirable	훌륭한	हुल्यूंगहान
Afraid	두려운	थुर्यऊन
Angry	화난	ह्वानान
Anxious	걱정되는	खकचग द्वेनन
Bad	나쁜	नाप्पुन
Bad	못된	मोत्वेन
Charming	매력적인	मर्यक जगीन
Complicated	복잡한	फोक्चाप–हान
Dazzling	눈부신	नूनवूशीन
Exciting	신나는	शीन्नानन
Gloomy	우울한	उऊलहान
Glorious	찬란한	छल्लानन्हान
Good	좋은	छोअन
Grateful	감사한	खामसाहान
Great	위대한	वीदेहान
Happy	행복한	हेंगबोकहान
Happy	기쁜	खीप्पुन
Humorous	웃기는	उक्कीनन
Inconvenient	불편한	फूल्फयनहान

Interesting	흥미로운	हुंगमीरोउन
Lonely	고독한	खोदोखान
Lonely	외로운	वेरोउन
Moving	감동적인	खाम्दोंग–जगीन
Peaceful	평화로운	फ्यन्गह्वा–रोउन
Pleasant	즐거운	छुलगउन
Pleasant	유쾌한	यूख्वेहान
Proud	자랑스러운	छारांगसरउन
Refreshing	상쾌한	संगख्वेहान
Sad	슬픈	सुल्फुन
Shameful	부끄러운	फूकुरउन
Simple	단순한	थानसूनहान
Sorry	미안한	मीआनहान
Sparkling	반짝거리는	फानचाक खरीनन
Stylish	멋있는	मशीनन
Tedious	지루한	छीरूहान
Terrible	무서운	मुसउन
Thankful	고마운	खोमाउन
Undeserved	억울한	अगुरहान
Unpleasant	불쾌한	फूलख्वेहान

Feelings

English	Hangeul	Pronunciation
Arduous	고된	खोद्वेन
Arduous	힘겨운	हीमगयऊन
Beautiful	아름다운	आरुम्दाउन
Brave	씩씩한	सीकसीखान
Careful	조심스러운	छोशीम–सरऊन
Clean	깨끗한	केकअथान
Clear	명확한	म्यंगह्वाखान
Close	가까운	खाकाउन
Comfortable	편안한	फयन्आनहान
Cute	귀여운	ख्वीयऊन
Dead	죽은	छूगुन
Definite	뚜렷한	तूर्‌यथान
Difficult	어려운	अर्‌यऊन
Dirty	더러운	थरउन
Easy	쉬운	श्वीन
Fresh	신선한	शीनसनहान
Good	착한	छाकखान
Hateful	미운	मीउन
Healthy	건강한	खनगांगहान

Hopeful	희망찬	हुइमांगदान
Live	살아있는	सारा–इन्नन
Lively	싱싱한	शींगशींगहान
Loose	헐거운	हलगउन
Loose	헐렁한	हल्लंगहान
Lovely	사랑스러운	सरांगसरउन
Messy	지저분한	छीजबुनहान
Neat	깔끔한	कालकमहान
Noisy	시끄러운	शीकुरऊन
Perfect	완벽한	वानबयखान
Pleased	만족스러운	मानजोक सरउन
Poor	서투른	सथूरुन
Positive	긍정적인	खुंगजंगजगीन
Powerful	힘있는	हीम–इन्नन
Pretty	예쁜	येप्पुन
Quite	조용한	छोयोंगहान
Shy	수줍은	सूजूबुन
Sick	아픈	आफुन
Sleepy	졸린	छोल्लीन
Smart	똑똑한	त्तोकतोखान
Sparse	엉성한	अंगसंगहान

Straight	반듯한	फान्अथान
Strong	튼튼한	थनथन–हान
Stupid	멍청한	मंगजंगहान
Tickling	간지러운	खानजीरउन
Tired	피곤한	फीगोनहान
Weak	약한	याकखान
Withered	시들은	शीदुरुन

Colors

English	Hangeul	Pronunciation
Black	검은	खमन
Blue	파란	फारान
Bright	밝은	फालगुन
Dark	어두운	अदुऊन
Dark	진한	छीनहान
Green	푸른	फूरुन
Light	연한	यन्हान
Red	빨간	पालगान
Red	붉은	फूल्गान
White	하얀	हायान
Yellow	노란	नोरान

Tastes

English	Hangeul	Pronunciation
Delicious	맛있는	माशीन्नन
Fatty	기름진	खीरूमजीन
Hot	매운	मेऊन
Mild	연한	यन्हान
Puckery	떫은	तल्बन
Refreshing	개운한	खेउनहान
Salty	짠	चान
Sour	신	शीन
Sweet	단	थान
Taste flat	싱거운	शीन्गाअउन
Tasteless	맛없는	माश–अम्नन
Tasty	고소한	खोशोहान
Thick	진한	छीनहान

Measurements

English	Hangeul	Pronunciation
Abundant	풍부한	फूंबूहान
Abundant	풍족한	फूंगजोखान
Appropriate	적당한	छकतांगहान
Big	큰	खुन
Chubby	통통한	थोंग्थोंगहान

Deep	깊은	खीप्फुन
Enough	넉넉한	नक्नक–हान
Far	먼	मन
Fat	뚱뚱한	तुंग्तुंगहान
Few	적은	छगन
High	높은	नोफुन
Lacking	부족한	फूजोखान
Long	긴	खिन
Low	낮은	नाजन
Many	많은	मानन
Narrow	좁은	छोबुन
Near	가까운	खाकाऊन
Needy	빈곤한	फीनगोनहान
Poor	가난한	खानानहान
Roomy	넓은	न्लबन
Shallow	얕은	यात्थुन
Short	짧은	चाल्बुन
Small	작은	छागुन
Thick	굵은	खुल्गुन
Thin	가는	खानुन
Thin	날씬한	नाल्सीनहान

Textures

English	Hangeul	Pronunciation
Angled	각진	खाक्चीन
Coarse	거친	खछीन
Cushiony	푹신한	फुक्शीन्हान

Damp	촉촉한	छोक्छोक–हान
Dry	건조한	खन्जोहान
Hard	딱딱한	ताक्ताक–हान
Oily	기름진	खीरुम्जीन
Round	동그란	थोंगुरान
Round	둥근	थुन्गुन
Sharp	뾰족한	प्योजोक–हान
Sharp	날카로운	नाल्खारोऊन
Smooth	미끄러운	मीकुरअऊन
Soft	부드러운	फुदुरऊन
Square	네모난	नेमोनान
Sticky	끈적한	कुन्जक–हान
Tender	연한	यन्हान
Wet	축축한	छुक्छुक–हान

Speeds

English	Hangeul	Pronunciation
Early	이른	ईरुन
Fast	빠른	पारुन
Hurried	서두른	सदूरुन
Late	늦은	नुजुन
Rapid	신속한	शिन्सोखान
Slow	천천히	छन्छनही
Urgent	급한	खुप्फान

Relationship

English	Hangeul	Pronunciation
Blind date	미팅	मिथिंग
Boyfriend	남자친구	नाम्जा छींगू
Boyfriend, girlfriend	애인	एईन
Breaking off engagement	파혼	फाहोन
Broken heart	실연	सीर्यन
Couple	연인	यनीन
Darling, honey, sweety	자기, 여보	छागी, यबो
Date	데이트	देइथु
Dating	연애	यने
Divorce	이혼	ईहोन
Engagement	약혼	याखोन
Girlfriend	여지친구	यजा छींगू
Marriage meeting	맞선	मात्सन
Second marriage	재혼	छेहोन
Wedding	결혼	ख्यरोन

Family Members

English	Hangeul	Pronunciation
Dad (Informal)	아빠	आप्पा

Elderly Man (Grandpa)	할아버지	हाराबजी
Elderly Woman (Grandmother)	할머니	हाल्मनी
Father	아버지	आबअजी
Father in law	시아버지	शी–आबजी
Father in law	장인어른	छांगीनअरुन
Mother	어머니	अमनी
Mother in law	시어머니	शी–अमनी
Mother in law	장모님	छांग्मोनीम
Mum	엄마	अम्मा
Older Brother (If the speaker is female)	오빠	ओप्पा
Older Brother (If the speaker is male)	형	ह्यंग
Uncle	아저씨	आजसी
Older Sister (If the speaker is female)	언니	अन्नी
Older Sister (If the speaker is male)	누나	नूना
Older Woman (Polite)	아주머니	आजुमनी
Older Woman (Less Polite)	아줌마	आजुम्मा
Younger Sibling (Regardless of speaker's gender)	동생	थोंगसेंग

Weekdays

English	Hangeul	Pronunciation
Sunday	일요일	इर्योइल
Monday	월요일	वर्योइल
Tuesday	화요일	ह्वायोइल
Wednesday	수요일	सुयोइल
Thursday	목요일	मोग्योइल
Friday	금요일	खुम्योइल
Saturday	토요일	थोयोइल

Months

English	Hangeul	Pronunciation
January	일월	इर–वल
February	이월	ई–वल
March	삼월	साम–वल
April	사월	सा–वल
May	오월	ओ–वल
June	유월	यू–वल
July	칠월	छीर–वल
August	팔월	फार–वल
September	구월	खू–वल
October	시월	शी–वल
November	십일월	शीप इर–वल
December	십이월	शीप ई–वल

Conjunction

English	Hangeul	Pronunciation
And	그리고	खुरीगो
Because	때문에	तेमुने
But	그러나	खुरअ–ना
But	그렇지만	खुरअ–छीमान
But	하지만	हाजीमान
Following	이어서	ईअस
However	아무리	आमूरी
In accordance with	따라서	तारासअ
So	그래서	खुरेसअ

Country Names

English	Hangeul	Pronunciation
Australia	호주	होजू
Austria	오스트리아	ओस्थुरिया
Brazil	브라질	फुराजील
Canada	캐나다	खेनादा
China (PRC)	중국	छुंगुक
China (Taiwan)	대만	थेमान
England (United Kingdom)	영국	यंगुक
France	프랑스	फुरांग्सु

Germany	독일	थोगील
Hong Kong	홍콩	होंगखोंग
India	인도	ईन्दो
Italy	이탈리아	ईथालीया
Japan	일본	ईल्बोन
Korea	한국	हांगुक
Malaysia	말레이지아	मालेइजिया
Mexico	멕시코	मेक्सीखो
Mongolia	몽고	मोंगो
Myanmar (Burma)	미얀마	मीआन्मा
New Zealand	뉴질랜드	न्यूजीलेन्द
North Korea	북한	फुखान
Singapore	싱가폴	शिंगापोल
South Korea	남한	नाम्हान
Spain	스페인	सुफेइन
Sweden	스웨덴	स्वीदेन
Switzerland	스위스	सुवीस
Thailand	태국	थेगुक
The Philippines	필리핀	फील्लीफीन
United States of America (USA)	미국	मीगुक
Vietnam	베트남	फेथउ–नाम

Continents

English	Hangeul	Pronunciation
Africa	아프리카	आफुरिखा
Asia	아시아	आशिआ
Europe	유럽	यूरप
North America	북아메리카	फुक आमेरिखा
Oceania	오세아니아	ओसेआनिआ
South America	남아메리카	नाम आमेरिखा

Oceans

English	Hangeul	Pronunciation
Pacific Ocean	태평양	थेफ्यंग्यांग
Atlantic Ocean	대서양	थेसअयांग
Indian Ocean	인도양	ईन्दोयांग
South Pole	남극	नाम्गुक
North Pole	북극	फुक्कुक

General Words

English	Hangeul	Pronunciation
Airport	공항	खोंगहांग
Aquarium	수족관	सुजोक्वान
Arboretum	수목원	सुमोग्वन
Beach	해변	हेब्यन

Beach	해수욕장	हेसूयोक्चांग
Bridge	다리	थारी
Broomstick	빗자루	फीच्चारू
Bus station	버스정류소	बसु छंग्नयूसो
Cave	동굴	थोंगुल
Call-bell	초인종	छोइन्जोंग
Concession	양보	यांग्बो
Crossroads	교차로	ख्योछारो
Crosswalk	횡단보도	ह्वेंगदान्बोदो
Danger	위험	वीहम
Distance	거리	खरी
Dolphin	돌고래	थोल्खोरे
Downhill	내리막	नेरीमाक
Dustpan	쓰레받기	सुरेफात्की
Exclusive bus lane	버스전용차로	बसुछन्योंग–छारो
Front	전방	छन्बांग
Fall	폭포	फोक्पो
Field	들	थुल
Floor cloth	걸레	खल्ले
Gate	문	मुन
Go slow	서행	सहेंग
Hill	언덕	अन्दक
Lake	호수	होशू

Large bridge	대교	थेग्यो
Lane	차선	छासन
Limit	제한	छेहान
Mountain	산	सान
Middle lane	중앙선	छुंगांग--सन
One-way street	일방통행	इल्बांग–थोंगहेंग
Otter	물개	मुल्गे
Parking	주차	छुछा
Parking lot	주차장	छुछाजांग
Prohibited	금지	खुम्जी
Protection	보호	फोहो
Palace	궁	खुंग
Park	공원	खोंग्वन
River	강	खांग
Rock	바위	फावी
Rock	암	आम
River-side road	강변도로	खांग्ब्यन–दोरो
Road	차로	छारो
Sea	바다	फादा
Section	구간	खुगान
Shark	상어	सांगअ
Signal	신호등	शिन्होदुंग

Sprayer	분무기	फुन्मुगी
Standing	정차	छंग्छा
Stop	정지	छंग्जी
Straight ahead	직진	छीक्चीन
Station	역	यक
Subway station	지하철역	छीहाछ्ल यक
Temple	사찰	साछाल
Temple	사원	सावन
Temple	절	छल
Ticket	표	फ्यो
Ticket machine	발권기	फाल–ग्वंगी
Ticket window	매표구	मेफ्योगू
Tower	탑	थाप
Traffic sign	교통표지판	ख्योथोंग–फ्योजीफान
Tunnel	터널	थनल
Train station	기차역	खीच्छा यक
Valley	계곡	ख्येगोक
Uphill	오르막	ओरुमाक
U-turn	유턴	युथन
Zone	구역	खुयक
Zoo	동물원	थोंग्मुल्वन

Transportation

English	Hangeul	Pronunciation
Airoplane	비행기	फीहैंगी
Bicycle	자전거	छाजंगअ
Bus	버스	बसु
Car	자동차	छादोंग–छा
Cultivator	경운기	ख्यंगुंगी
Line number	호선	होसन
Motorcycle	오토바이	ओथोबाई
Passenger car	승용차	सुंग्योंग–छा
Ship	배	फे
Subway	지하철 (전철)	छीहाछल (छनछल)
Taxi	택시	थैक्सी
Tractor	트랙터	थरेक्थअ
Train	기차 (열차)	खीच्छा

Directions

English	Hangeul	Pronunciation
East	동	थोंग
Left	좌	छ्वा
Left side	좌측	छ्वाछुक
North	북	फुक

Right	우	उ
Right side	우측	उछुक
South	남	नाम
Turn left	좌회전	छवाह्वेजन
Turn right	우회전	उह्वेजन
West	서	स

Places

English	Hangeul	Pronunciation
Airport	공항	खोंगहांग
Airstrip	활주로	ह्वाल–जुरो
Dining-car	식당차	सीक्तांग–छा
Gas (petrol) station	주유소	छुयुसो
Guesthouse	민박	मीन्बाक
Hotel	호텔	होथेल
Inn	여관	यग्वान
Luggage chamber	짐칸	छिम्खान
Platform	승강장	सुंगांग–जांग
Port	항	हांग
Port	항구	हांगु
Repair shop	정비소	छंग्बीसो

Sleeping car	침대차	छीम्दे—छा
Station	정류소	छंग्न्यूसो
Subway station	전철역	छन्छर—यक
Ticket office	매표소	मेफ्योसो
Train station	기차역	खीच्छा—यक

Clothes

English	Hangeul	Pronunciation
Blouse	블라우스	फ्लाउसु
Blue jeans	청바지	छंग—फाजी
Breeches	바지	फाजी
Cardigan	가디건	खादीगन
Clothes	옷	ओत
Coat	코트	खोथु
Cotton pants	면바지	म्यन—फाजी
Dress shirt	남방셔츠	नामबांग स्यछु
Full dress	정장	छंग्जांग
Jacket	상의/잠바	सांगुई / छाम्बा
Jacket	자켓	छाखेत
Jumper	잠바	छाम्बा

Knitted clothes	니트	नीथु
Korean dress	한복	हान्बोक
Long sleeve	긴팔	खिन्फाल
One-piece dress	원피스	वन–फीसु
Pajamas	잠옷	छामोत
Shirt	셔츠	स्यछु
Short sleeve	반팔	फान्फाल
Skirt	치마	छीमा
Sports wear	운동복	उन्दोंग–बोक
Suit	양복	यांग–बोक
Sweater	스웨터	सुवेथअ
Trousers	하의	हाउई
Underwear	속옷	सोगोत
Underwear	내복	नेबोक
Uniform	제복	छेबोक
Vest	조끼	छोक्की
Working uniform	작업복	छागप–बोक

Accesories

English	Hangeul	Pronunciation
Belt	허리띠	हरीती
Belt	혁대	ह्यक्तै

Braces	멜빵	मेल्पांग
Gloves	장갑	छांगाप
Hat	모자	मोजा
Muffler	머플러	मफुलअ
Scarf	목도리	मोक्तोरी

Animals

English	Hangeul	Pronunciation
Antelope	영양	यंग्यांग
Bear	곰	खोम
Camel	낙타	नाक्था
Cat	고양이	खोयांगी
Cheetah	치타	छीथा
Chicken	닭	थाक
Chimpanzee	침팬지	छीम्फेन्जी
Cow	소	सो
Deer	사슴	सासुम
Dog	개	खे
Fox	여우	यऊ
Giraffe	기린	खिरीन
Goat	염소	यम्सो
Gorilla	고릴라	खोरिल्ला

Hippo	하마	हामा
Horse	말	माल
Hyena	하이에나	हाइएना
Koala bear	코알라	खोआल्ला
Leopard	표범	फ्योबम
Lion	사자	साजा
Mole	두더지	थुदअजी
Monkey	원숭이	वन्सुंगी
Orangutan	오랑우탄	ओरांगुथान
Panda	팬더	फेन्दअ
Pig	돼지	थ्वेजी
Pony	조랑말	छोरांग–माल
Rabbit	토끼	थोक्की
Raccoon	너구리	नगूरी
Rat	쥐	छवी
Rhinoceros	코뿔소	खोप्पुल–सो
Sheep	양	यांग
Squirrel	다람쥐	थाराम–छवी
Tiger	호랑이	होरांगी
Whale	고래	खोरे
Wolf	늑대	नुक्ते
Zebra	얼룩말	अल्लुक–माल

Reptiles

English	Hangeul	Pronunciation
Big snake	구렁이	खुरंगी
Crocodile	악어	आगअ
Frog	개구리	खेगुरी
Iguana	이구아나	इगुआना
Lizard	도마뱀	थोमा–फेम
Snake	뱀	फेम
Turtle	거북이	खबुगी

Birds

English	Hangeul	Pronunciation
Crane	두루미	थुरुमी
Crow	까마귀	कामाख्वी
Dove	비둘기	फीदुल्गी
Duck	오리	ओरी
Eagle	독수리	थोक्सुरी
Goose	거위	खवी
Gull	갈매기	खाल्मेगी
Magpie	까치	क्काछी
Ostrich	타조	थाजो

Parrot	앵무새	एंग–मुसे
Peacock	공작	खोंग्जाक
Penguin	펭귄	फेंग्वीन
Sparrow	참새	छाम्से
Stork	황새	ह्वांग्से
Swan	백조	फेक्चो

Home Related

English	Hangeul	Pronunciation
Basement	지하실	छीहाशील
Bathroom	욕실	योक–शील
Bedroom	침실	छीम्शील
Bed	침대	छीम्दे
Boiler room	보일러실	फोइलअ–शील
Bookcase	책장	छेक्चांग
Chair	의자	उइजा
Clothes chest	장농	छांगनोंग
Clothes chest	옷장	ओत्चांग
Coat hanger	옷걸이	ओत्खरी
Ceiling	천장	छन्जांग
Closet	다락	थाराक

Court	마당	मादांग
Counter	싱크대	सींग–खुदे
Desk	책상	छेक्सांग
Drawer	서랍	सराप
Floor	마루	मारु
Garage	차고	छागो
Garden	정원	छंग्वन
House	집	छीप
Kitchen	주방	छुबांग
Living room	거실	खशील
Master bedroom	안방	आन्बांग
Porch	현관	ह्यन–ग्वान
Pantry chest	찬장	छान्जांग
Roof	옥상	ओक्सांग
Shelf	선반	सन्बान
Study	서재	सजे
Table	식탁	सीत्ताक
Toilet	화장실	ह्वाजांग–शील
Vanity	화장대	ह्वाजांग्दे
Veranda	베란다	फेरान्दा
Warehouse	창고	छांगो

Electronics

English	Hangeul	Pronunciation
Clock	시계	सीगे
Computer	컴퓨터	खम्फ्यूथअ
Electric cattle	전기주전자	छंगीछुजन्जा
Electronic heating pad	전기장판	छंगीजांग्फान
Electronic shaver	전기면도기	छंगीम्यन्दोगी
Gas range	가스렌지	खासुरेन्जी
Iron	다리미	थारीमी
Microwave oven	전자렌지	छन्जारेन्जी
Mixer	믹서기	मीक्सगी
Oven	오븐	ओबुन
Refrigerator	냉장고	नेंग्जांगो
Stove	스토브	सुथोबु
Telephone	전화기	छन्ह्वागी
Television	텔레비전	थेल्लेबीजन
Vacuum cleaner	청소기	छंगसोगी
Washing machine	세탁기	सेथाक्की

Kitchen Related

English	Hangeul	Pronunciation
Apron	앞치마	आप–छीमा
Balance	저울	घऊल
Chef's knife	채칼	छेखाल
Chopping board	도마	थोमा
Chopsticks	젓가락	छत्काराक
Cup	컵	खप
Dish	접시	छप्सी
Dish cloth	행주	हेंग्जू
Earthen bowl	뚝배기	तुक्पेगी
Frying pan	후라이팬	हुराइफेन
Grater	강판	खांग्फान
Kettle	주전자	छुजन्जा
Knife	칼	खाल
Ladle	국자	खुक्चा
Pot	냄비	नेम्बी
Rice pot	밥솥	फाप्सोत
Rubber gloves	고무장갑	खोमु–छांगाप
Scrubber	수세미	सुसेमी

Spatula	뒤집개	थ्वीजीप्के
Spoon	숟가락	सुत्काराक
Tray	쟁반	छेंग्बान
Vessel	그릇	खुरुत
Weighing machine	계량기	ख्येरांगी

Bathroom Related

English	Hangeul	Pronunciation
Bathtub	욕조	योक्यो
Dentifrice	치약	छीयाक
Gourd	바가지	फागाजी
Razor	면도기	म्यन्दोगी
Shampoo	샴푸	श्याम्फू
Soap	비누	फीनू
Tap	수도꼭지	सुदोकोक्ची
Toilet	화 장 실	हवाजांग–शील
Toothbrush	칫솔	छीसोल
Towel	수건	सुगन
Washbasin	세숫대야	सेसुतेया
Washstand	세면대	सेम्यन्दे

Season

English	Hangeul	Pronunciation
Autumn	가을	खाउल
Early fall	초가을	छो–खाउल
Early spring	초봄	छो–फोम
Early summer	초여름	छो–यरुम
Early winter	초겨울	छो–ख्यऊल
Late fall	늦가을	नुत्खाउल
Late spring	늦봄	नुत्पोम
Late summer	늦여름	नुत्यरुम
Late winter	늦겨울	नुत्ख्यऊल
Midsummer	한여름	हान्यरुम
Midwinter	한겨울	हान्ख्यऊल
Spring	봄	फोम
Summer	여름	यरुम
Winter	겨울	ख्यऊल

Colors

English	Hangeul	Pronunciation
Black	검정색	खम्जंग–सेक
Blue	파랑색	फारांग–सेक
Blue	청색	छंग–सेक
Crimson	진홍색	छीन्होंग–सेक

Deep blue	남색	नाम–सेक
Deep red	다홍색	थाहोंग–सेक
Golden	금색	खुम–सेक
Gray	회색	ह्वे–सेक
Green	초록색	छोरोक–सेक
Green	녹색	नोक–सेक
Light green	연두색	यन्दू–सेक
Maroon	밤색	फाम–सेक
Orange	주황색	छुह्वांग–सेक
Purple	보라색	फोरा–सेक
Red	빨강색	पाल्गांग–सेक
Silver	은색	उन–सेक
Sky blue	하늘색	हानुल–सेक
White	흰색	हुइन–सेक
Yellow	노랑색	नोरांग–सेक

General Words for Foods

English	Hangeul	Pronunciation
Alcoholic drink	술	सुल
Beef	소고기	सो–खोगी
Bread	빵	पांग
Brown seaweed	미역	मीयक
Chicken	닭고기	थाक–खोगी

Cookie	과자	ख्वाजा
Dried laver	김	खिम
Fish	생선	शैंग्सन
Kimchi	김치	किमछी
Grilled pancake	전	छन
Herbs or wild greens	나물	नामुल
Hard-boiled food	조림	छोरीम
Kelp	다시마	थाशीमा
Meat	고기	खोगी
Pork	돼지고기	थेगी–खोगी
Raw fish	회	हे
Rice	밥	फाप
Rice cake	떡	तक
Rice topped with other ingredients	덮밥	थप्पाप
Rice served in soup	국밥	खुक्पाप
Steamed dish	찜	चीम
Stew	전골	छंगोल
Soup	죽	छुक
Soup	국	खुक
Stew	탕	थांग
Stew	찌개	चीगे
Tea	차	छा

Grilled Foods

English	Hangeul	Pronunciation
Barbecued beef	불고기	फुल्गोगी
Broiled beef tripe and chitterlings	양곱창구이	यांगोप–छांगुई
Broiled eel	장어구이	छांगअ–गुई
Broiled flatfish	가자미구이	खाजामी–गुई
Broiled short ribs	갈비구이	खाल्बी–गुई
Broiled Spanish mackerel	삼치구이	साम्छी–गुई
Grilled chicken	닭구이	थाक–गुई
Grilled fish	생선구이	शेंगसन–गुई
Grilled side of pork	삼겹살구이	सांग्यप्साल–गुई
Grilled sirloin	등심구이	थुंग्सीम–गुई
Grilled tenderloin	안심구이	आन्सीम–गुई
Grilled toduk root	더덕구이	थदक्कुई
Seasoned and grilled yellow dried pollack	황태구이	ह्वांग्थे–गुई

Kimchi Types

English	Hangeul	Pronunciation
Chopped radish kimchi	깍두기	कात्तुगी

Ponytail kimchi	총각김치	छोंगाक–किमची
Red water kimchi	나박김치	नाबाक–किमची
Rolled kimchi	보쌈김치	फोसाम–किमची
Summer green water kimchi	열무물김치	यल्मुमुल–किमची
White cabbage kimchi	백김치	फेक–किमची
Whole cabbage kimchi	배추김치	फेछू–किमची
Winter white water kimchi	동치미	थोंग–छीमी

Meat Dishes

English	Hangeul	Pronunciation
Barbecued beef	불고기	फुल्गोगी
Beef boiled in soy	장조림	छांग्जोरीम
Broiled short ribs	갈비구이	खाल्बी–गुई
Chicken	통닭	थोंग्थाक
Ginseng chicken soup	삼계탕	साम्ग्येथांग
Grilled side of pork	삼겹살구이	सांग्यप्साल–गुई
Grilled sirloin	등심구이	थुंग्सीम–गुई
Grilled tenderloin	안심구이	आन्सीम–गुई
Korean sausage	순대	सुन्दे

Pork hock	족발	छोक्पाल
Seasoned shredded beef	육회	यूख्वे
Slices of boiled pork	편육	फ्यन्यूक
Variety vegetable wrap with rice and meat	보쌈	फोस्साम

Noodles Dishes

English	Hangeul	Pronunciation
Buckwheat noodles	메밀국수	मेमील–खुक्सू
Buckwheat noodles with clear chicken soup	막국수	माकुक्सू
Buckwheat noodles with raw fish	회냉면	ह्वेनेंग–म्यन
Cold noodles in soup	냉면	नेंग–म्यन
Handmade noodles	칼국수	खाल्कुक्सू
Hot spicy noodles	쫄면	चोन्म्यन
Japanese noodles	우동	उदोंग
Mixed vegetables with noodles	잡채	छाप्चे
Noodle casserole	국수전골	खुक्सू–छंगोल

Noodles in soy bean water	냉콩국수	नेंग–खोंग–खुक्सू
Ramyon	라면	राम्यन
Spicy buckwheat noodles	비빔냉면	फिबिम–नेंग–म्यन
Watery buck wheat noodles	물냉면	मुल–नेंग–म्यन
Wheat flour noodles	국수	खुक्सू

Rice Dishes

English	Hangeul	Pronunciation
Boiled rice mixed with vegetables	돌솥밥	थोल्सोत–फाप
Boiled rice with various nutritious ingredients	영양밥	यंग्यांग–फाप
Broiled scorched rice	누룽지밥	नुरूंग्जी–फाप
Five-grain rice	오곡밥	ओखोक–फाप
Fried rice	볶음밥	फोकुम–फाप
Kimchi fried rice	김치볶음밥	किमची फोकुम–फाप
Mixed vegetables on rice	비빔밥	फीबीमफाप
Rice ball	주먹밥	छुमक–फाप
Rice wrapped in seaweed	김밥	खिम–फाप

Sizzling vegetables on rice	돌솥비빔밥	थोल्सोत फीबीमफाप
Stir-fried octopus	낙지볶음밥	नाक्ची फोकुम–फाप

Sea food Dishes

English	Hangeul	Pronunciation
Abalone porridge	전복죽	छन्बोक्चुक
Blue crab marinatet in soy sauce	간장게장	खिन्जांग–खेजांग
Blue crab stew	꽃게탕	कोत–खेथांग
Boiled down hairtail	갈치조림	खाल्छी–छोरीम
Broiled eel	장어구이	छांगअ–गुई
Broiled flatfish	가자미구이	खाजीमी–गुई
Broiled Spanish mackerel	삼치구이	साम्छी–गुई
Grilled fish	생선구이	शेंग्सन–गुई
Hot spicy fish soup	매운탕	मेउन–थांग
Mixed raw skate and vegetables with seasoning	홍어회무침	होंगअ–हेमु–छीम
Octopus stew	낙지전골	नाक्ची–चंगोल
Seasoned and grilled yellow dried pollack	황태구이	हवांग्थे–गुई

Spicy bai top shells with mixed vegertables	골뱅이무침	खोल्बेंगी–मुछीम
Stir-fried octopus	낙지볶음	नाक्ची–फोक्कुम

Soup

English	Hangeul	Pronunciation
Bean sprout soup	콩나물국	खोंग्नामुल–खुक
Blue crab stew	꽃게탕	कोक्के–थांग
Boiled chicken stuffed with rice and ginseng	닭백숙	थाक्बेकसुक
Chilled cucumber soup	오이냉국	ओई–नेंग–खुक
Dried pollack soup	북어국	फुगअ–खुक
Dumpling soup	만두국	मान्दु–खुक
Ginseng chicken soup	삼계탕	साम्ग्ये–थांग
Hot spicy fish soup	매운탕	मेऊन–थांग
Hot spicy stew soup	육개장	युक्के–थांग
Knuckle bone soup	도가니탕	थोगानी–थांग
Loach and bean paste soup	추어탕	छुअथांग
Ox bone and stew meat stock soup	설렁탕	सल्लंग–थांग

Ox short rib soup	갈비탕	खाल्बी–थांग
Ox tail soup	꼬리곰탕	कोरीखोम–थांग
Potato soup	감자탕	खाम्जा–थांग
Rice cake soup	떡국	तक्कुक
Sea mustard in chilled vinegar water	미역냉국	मियक–नेंग–थांग
Sea mustard soup	미역국	मियक–खुक
Seafood soup	해물탕	हेमुल–थांग
Spicy fish egg soup	알탕	आल्थांग
Stew meat and tripe soup	곰탕	खोम–थांग
Sunrise soup	해장국	हेजांग–खुक

Stews

English	Hangeul	Pronunciation
Army base stew	부대찌개	फुदे–चीगे
Bean paste stew	된장찌개	थ्वेन्जांग–चीगे
Beef and vegetable stew	소고기전골	सोखोगी–चंगोल
Beef rib and octopus casserole	갈낙전골	खाल्लाक–चंगोल
Fairy casserole	신선로	शीन्सन–चंगोल
Fast fermented bean paste stew	청국장찌개	छंगुक्चांग–चीगे

Kimchi casserole	김치전골	किमची–चंगोल
Kimchi stew	김치찌개	किमची–चीगे
Octopus stew	낙지전골	नाक्ची–चंगोल
Raw bean curd stew	순두부찌개	सुन्दुबु–चीगे
Seasoned entrails and vegetable stew	곱창전골	खोप्चांग–चंगोल
Short rib stew	갈비찜	खाल्बीचीम

Stir-fried/Fried Foods & Pancakes

English	Hangeul	Pronunciation
Flat cake	부침개	फुछीम्गे
Green-bean (lentil) pancake	빈대떡	फिन्दे–तक
Kimchi fried rice	김치볶음	किमची–फोक्कुम
Pancake with welsh onion	파전	फाजन
Pan-fried kimchi with flour	김치전	किमची–जन
Pan-fried meat	고기전	खोगी–जन
Potato pancake	감자전	खाम्जा–जन
Sauteed mush-room salad	버섯볶음	फसत–फोक्कुम
Stir-fried octopus	낙지볶음	नाक्ची–फोक्कुम

Snacks

English	Hangeul	Pronunciation
Deep fried dough stuffed with vegetables and others	고로케	खोरोखे
Deep fried foods	튀김	थ्वीगीन
Deep fried sweet potato with syrup	맛탕	मात्तांग
Dumplings	만두	मान्दू
Korean sausage	순대	सुन्दे
Pancake stuffed with brown sugar, cinnamon, and nuts etc...	호떡	होत्तक
Rice wrapped in seaweed	김밥	खिम्फाप
Stir fried rice cake	떡볶기	तक्पोक्की

Western Dishes

English	Hangeul	Pronunciation
Beef cutlet	비프까스	फीफअ–कास
Chicken cutlet	치킨까스	छीखीन–कास
Curry and rice	카레라이스	खारे–राइस
Fish cutlet	생선까스	शेंग्सन–कास
Hamburger made with bulgogi meat	불고기버거	फुल्गोगी–फगअ

Lobster	바닷가재	फादाक्काजे
Mushroom gratin	버섯그라탕	फसत–खुराथांग
Pork cutlet	돈까스	थोन्कास
Rice with shrimp and mozzarella cheese	새우도리아	सेऊदोरिआ

Drinks

English	Hangeul	Pronunciation
Beer	맥주	मेक्चू
Black tea	홍차	होंग–छा
Clear soda pop	사이다	साइदा
Fruit punch made of honey	수정과	सुजंग्वा
Green tea	녹차	नोक–छा
Ice coffee	냉커피	नेंग–खफ़ी
Ice flakes with syrup	빙수	फिंग्सु
Korean distilled liquor	소주	सोजु
Raw rice wine	막걸리	माक्कल्ली
Sweet drink made from fermented rice	식혜	शिख्ये
Wine	포도주	फोदोजु

KOREAN HOLIDAYS/SEASONS

Special Days

English	Date	Hangeul
15th day of the 1st lunar month	Lunar calendar 1/15	정월대보름 छंग्वल-थेफोरूम
3rd day of the 3rd lunar month	Lunar calendar 3/3	삼짇날 साम्जीन्नाल
105th day after	105th day after	한식
15th day of the 6th lunar month	Lunar calendar 6/15	유두 युदू
Hottest period of summer	Mid-July to mid-August	삼복 साम्बोक
7th day of the 7th lunar month	Lunar calendar 7/7	칠석 छील्सक
Armed Forces Day	1-Oct	국군의날 खुक्कूने-नाल
Anniversary of March 1st Independence Movement.	1-Mar	삼일절 सामिल-जल
Arbor Day	5-Apr	식목일 सींग-मोगील
Buddha's Birthday	Lunar calendar 4/8	석가탄신일 (सक्काथान्सीन-इल)
Constitution Day	17-Jul	제헌절

		छेहन-जल
Christmas	25-Dec	성탄절
		संग्थान-जल
Children's Day	5-May	어린이날
		अरीनी-नाल
Harvest Moon	Lunar calendar	추석
Festival	8/15	छूसक
Independence day		독립기념일
(other countries)		थोंग्नीप-खीन्यम-इल
Lunar New Year	Lunar calendar	설
	1/1	सल
Labor Day	1-May	노동절
		नोदोंग-जल
Liberation day	15-Aug	광복절
		ख्वांग्बोक-जल
Memorial Day.	6-Jun	현충일
		हान्छुंग-इल
National holiday		국경일
		खुक्यंग-इल
National Foundation	3-Oct	개천절
Day		खेछन-जल
Parent's Day	8-May	어버이날
		अबई-नाल
Proclamation Day	9-Oct	한글날

		हांगुल-नाल
Teacher's Day	15-May	스승의날
		सुसुंगे-नाल
U.S. Thanksgiving	4th Thursday in	추수감사절
	November	छूसूगाम्साजल
Winter solstice	Dongji	हान्शीक
Tano	Lunar calendar	단오
	5/5	थानो
Winter solstice	22-Dec	동지
		थोंग्ची

Historical Places

English	Hangeul	Pronunciation
<u>Seoul</u>		
Dongnimmun	독립문	थोंगनीप-मुन
Memorial Hall	국립묘지	खुंग्नीप-म्योजी
Namsangol Tradi-	남산골 전통	नाम्सांगोल छन्थोंग
tional Folk Village	민속 마을	मीन्सोक माऊल
Seodaemun Prison	서대문 형무소	सदेमुन ह्यग-मूसो
<u>Gyeonggi Province/Incheon</u>		
Haengju Mountain Fortress	행주 산성	हेग्जू सान्संग
Korean Folk Village	한국민속촌	हांगुक-मीन्सोक्छोन
Panmunjeom	판문점	फान्मुन्जम
Site of Goryeo Palace	고려왕궁터	खोर्यअ वांगुंग्थअ

South chungchong Province / Daejeon

Chunghyon Sowon 충현서원 छुनह्यनसवन
(memorial hall for the great scholars and loyal subjects of the past)

Hwangsae Bawi 황새바위 हांग्से बाबी
(rock)Catholic Martyrdom Site 카톨릭 순교지 खाथेलीक सुंग्योजी

Kongju Hyanggyo 공주향교 खोंग्जु-हांग्यो
(local school annexed to the Confucian shrine)

Manharu (pavilion) 만하루 मान्हारू

Ssangsujong (pavilion) 쌍수정 सांग्सुजंग

Tomb of Gen. Kim Chong-so 김종서 장군 무덤 खिम जोंग-स छांगुन मुदम

Tomb of King Mur-yong 무녕왕릉 मून्यंग-वांगरूंग

Yonji (pond) 연지 यन्जी

North Gyeongsang Province / Daegu / Gyeongju

Andong Folk Village 안동 민속촌 आन्दोंग मीन्सोक-छोन

Cheonmachong 천마총 छन्माछोंग

Hahoe Folk Village 하회 민속촌 हाहे मीन्सोक-छोन

Seogbinggo (Ice Storage) 석빙고 सक्पीन्गो

Gyeongsang Province / Busan

Deokcheon Seowon 덕천서원 थक्छन सवन

Mun Ikjeom 문익점 मूनीक्चम
(First Cotton Cultivation)

Okjeon Tumuli	옥전 고분군	ओक्छन खोबून्गून
Tomb of King Suro	김수로왕릉	किम सुरो वांग रूंग
Tomb of Queen Suro	김수로왕비릉	किम सुरो वांगबी रूंग
U.N. Cemetery	UN 묘지	यू एन म्योजी
Yungong-dan	윤공단	यून्योंग-दान

Jeolla Province / Gwangju

Jiri-san Combat Memorial	지리산 전투 기념관	छीरीसान छन्थु खीन्यमग्वान
Nagan Folk Village	낙안 민속마을	नागान मेन्सोंग माऊल

North Chunchong Province

Chungnyeol-sa Shrine	충렬사	छूंगरयत्सा
Deokju Sanseong	덕주산성	थक्चू सान्संग
Jungang Pagoda	중앙탑	छुगांग्थ्याप
Relocation of Cheongpung Cultural Properties	청풍 문화재 단지	छंग्फूंग मून्ह्वाजे थान्जी

Jeju Island

Jeju Folk Village	민속촌	छेजू मीन्सोक्छोन
Residence of Kim, Cheong-hi	김정희 유배지	किम जंग ही यूबेजी
Samseonghyeol	삼성혈	साम्संग-ह्यल

Seongeup Folk Village	성읍 민속촌	संगूप मीन्सोक्छोन

Royal Places

English	Hangeul	Pronunciation
Seoul		
Deoksu Palace	덕수궁	थक्सु-गुंग
Unhyeon Palace	운현궁	उन्हयन-गुंग
Gyeongbok Palace	경복궁	ख्यंगबोक-गुंग
Changdeok Palace (Biwon Garden)	창덕궁 (비원)	छांग्दक गुंग
Changgyeong Palace	창경궁	छांग्यंग-गुंग
Gyeonghui Palace	경희궁	ख्यंगही-गुंग
Jongmyo Shrine	종묘	छोंग्म्यो
Incheon		
Yongheung Palace	용흥궁	योंगहंग-गुंग

Temples

English	Hangeul	
Seoul		
Jogye-sa	조계사	छोग्येसा
Hwagye-sa	화계사	ह्वायेसा
Bongwon-sa	봉원사	फोंग-वन्सा
Bongeun-sa	봉은사	फोंगुन्सा
Incheon		
Jeondeung-sa	전등사	छन्दुंग्सा

South Chungchong Province / Daejeon

Hyeonchung-sa	한중사	हान्छुंग्सा
Yongun-sa	용운사	योंगुन्सा

North Gyeongsang Province / Daegu / Gyeongju

Bunhwang-sa	분황사	फुन्हांग्सा
Bulguk-sa	불국사	फुल्गुक्सा
Donghwa-sa	동화사	थोंगह्वासा
Dori-sa	도리사	थोरीसा
Eunmun-sa	운문사	उन्मुन्सा
Eunjeok-sa	은적사	उन्जक्सा
Golgul-sa	골굴사	खोल्गूल्सा
Hwangryong-sa	황룡사	हांग-रयोंग्सा
Samjeon Grotto Temple	삼전굴사	साम्जं-गुल्सा
Songnim-sa	송림사	सोंग्नीम्सा
Tongilyak-sa	통일약사	थोंगीऌ याक्सा

Souht Gyeongsang Province / Busan

Beomeo-sa	범어사	फ्मअसा
Daewon-sa	대원사	थंवन्सा
Gilsang-am	길상암	खील्सांगाम्
Haein-sa	해인사	हेईन्सा
Naewon-sa	내원사	नेवन्सा
Seognam-sa	석남사	संग्नाक्सा

Ssanggye-sa	쌍계사	सांग्येसा
Thongdo-sa	통도사	थोंग्दोसा
Haein-sa	해인사	हेईन्स
Yonggung-sa	용궁사	योंगुंग्सा

Jeolla Province / Gwangju

Cheoneun-sa	천은사	छनुन्सा
Daedun-sa	대둔사	थेदुन्सा
Hwaom-sa	화엄사	हाअम्सा
Seonam-sa	선암사	सनाम्सा
Silsang-sa	실상사	शील्सांग्सा
Songgwang-sa	송광사	सोंग्वाग्सा
Yeongok-sa	연곡사	यंगोक्सा

North Chungchong Province

Mireuk-sa	미륵사	मीरूक्सा
Beopju-sa	법주사	फप्चुसा

Gyeonggi Province

Naksan-sa	낙산사	नाक्सान्सा
Sinheung-sa	신흥사	शीन्हुंग्सा

Jeju Island

Yakcheon-sa	약천사	यक्छन्सा
Cheonwhang-sa	천황사	छन्ह्वांग्सा

SHOPPING AREAS

English	Hangeul	Pronunciation
Central City	센트럴 시티	सेन्थुरल शीथी
COEX Mall	COEX 상가	कोएक्स सांगा
Dongdaemun Market	동대문 시장	थोंग-देमुन शीजांग
Garak-dong Agricultural Market	가락동 농수산물 시장	खाराक्तोंग नोंग्सु सान्मूल शीजों
Gyeong-dong Oriental Medicine Market	경동 한약시장	ख्यंग्दोंग हान्याक शीजांग
Hwanghak-dong Flea Market	황학동 벼룩시장	हवांगहात्तोंग फ्यरूक शीजांग
Insa-dong Shopping Area	인사동 상가	इन्सादोंग सांगा
Itaewon-dong Shopping Area	이태원 상가	इथेवन सांगा
Janganpyeong Antique Market	장안평 골동품 상가	छांगानफ्यंग खोल्दोगफुम सांगा
Myeong-dong Shopping Area	명동 쇼핑가	म्यंग्दोंग शॉफिंगा
Namdaemun Market	남대문 시장	नाम-देमुन शीजांग

Nonhyeon Furniture Street	논현동 가구거리	नोन्हानदोंग खागू खरी
Noryangjin Fish Market	노량진 수산 시장	नोरयांग्जीन सुसान शीजांग
Rodeo Street	로데오거리	रोदेओ-खरी
Wholesale Plant and Flower Market	지하 식물/꽃 시장	छीहा सीग्मुल/कोत शीजांग
Yangjae Flower Market	양재 꽃 시장	यांगजे कोत्त शीजांग
Yongsan Electronics Market	용산 전자상가	योंग्सान छन्जा सांगा

Major Museums

English	Hangeul	Pronunciation
Agricultural Museum	농업 박물관	नोंअप फांग्मुल्वान
Kimchi Museum	김치박물관	किमछी फांग्मुल्वान
National Folk Museum	국립 민속 박물관	थोंगनीप मीन्सोक फांग्मुल्वान
Seoul Historical Museum	서울 역사 박물관	सऊल यक्सा फांग्मुल्वान
Seoul Railway Museum	서울 철도박물관	सऊल छल्दो फांग्मुल्वान
War Museum	전쟁기념관	छन्जेंग खीन्यमग्वान

Major Landmarks

English	Hangeul	Pronunciation
Bukhan Mountain Fortress	북한산성	फुखान्सान-संग
Cheonggwonsa Shrine	청권사 무덤	छंग्वन्सा मुदम
China Town	차이나타운	छाइना थाउन
Cheongdong Theater	정동극장	छंगदोंग खुक्चांग
COEX Center	COEX 센터	कोएक्स सेन्थअ
Dream Land	드림랜드	थुरीम लेन्द
Dongdaemun	동대문	थोंगदेमुन
Ever Land	에버랜드	एबअ-लेन्द
Gimpo Airport	김포공항	किम्फो खोंगहांग
Gyeongbok Palace	경복궁	ख्यन्बोकुंग
Han River Boat Cruise	한강 유람선	हांगांग यूराम्सन
Incheon International Airport	인천국제공항	इन्छन खुक्चे खोंगहांग
Korea Life Insurance (KLI) 63 Building	63 빌딩	यूक्साम बिल्दींग
Korea World Trade Center	한국종합무역센터	हांगुक छुंगहाप मुयक सेन्थअ
Korea House	한국의 집	हांगुगे छीप
Little Angels Performing Arts Center	리틀엔젤스 예술회관	लीथुल एन्जेल्स येसुल हेग्वान
Lotte World	롯데월드	लोत्ते वल्द

Myeongdong Cathedral	명동 대성당	म्यंगदोग थेसंगदांग
Namdaemun (Great South Gate)	남대문	नाम्देमुन
National Theater of Korea	국립극장	खुंग्नीप खुक्चांग
Seoul Arts Center	서울 아트센터	सऊल आथु सेन्थअ
Seoul Land	서울랜드	सऊल लेन्द
Seoul Station	서울역	सऊल यक
Seoul Tower	서울 타워	सऊल थावअ
Suwon Mountain fortress	수원화성	सुवन्ह्वासंग
Yeongjong Island	영종도	यंगजोंग-दो
Yeouido	여의도	यइदो

Major Valleys / Islands / Beaches

English	Hangeul	Pronunciation
Ganghwa Island	강화도	खांगह्वा
Gwangalli Beach	광안리 해수욕장	ख्वांगाली हेसुयोक्चांग
Haeundae Beach	해운대 해수욕장	हेउन्दे हेसुयोक्चांग
Hamdeok Beach	함덕 해수욕장	हाम्दक हेसुयोक्चांग
Hyeopjae Beach	협재 해수욕장	हाप्चे हेसुयोक्चांग
Seongmo Island	석모도	संग्मो-दो
Songchu Valley	송추계곡	सोंग्छुख्येगोक
Songjeong Beach	송정 해수욕장	सोंग्जंग हेसुयोक्चांग
Wando Port	완도	वान्दो
Wŏlmi Isla	월미도	वल्मी-दो
Yeongjong Island	영종도	यंग्जोंदो

Schools

English	Hangeul	Pronunciation
Community collage	전문대학교	छल्मुन हाक्या
Day-care center	어린이집	अरिनीछीप
Elementary school	초등학교	छोदुंग हाक्यो
Graduate school	대학원	देहाग्वन
High school	고등학교	खोदुंग हाक्यो
Kindergarten	유치원	यूछीवन
Middle school	중학교	छुंग हाक्यो
University/college	대학교	देहाक्यो

Subjects

English	Hangeul	Pronunciation
Accounting	회계학	ह्वेग्ये-हाक
Anthropology	인류학	इल्यू-हाक
Aarchaeology	고고학	खोगो-हाक
Architectural engineering	건축공학	खन्चुक-खोग-हाक
Astronomy	천문학	छन्मुन-हाक
Biochemistry	생화학	सेंग-ह्वा-हाक
Bioengineering	생체공학	सेंग्छे-खोग-हाक
Biology	생물	सेंग्मुल
Biotechnology	생명공학	सेंग्म्यंग-हाक
Business administration	경영학	ख्यंग्यंग-हाक
Chemical engineering	화학공학	ह्वाहाक-खोंग-हाक
Chemistry	화학	ह्वाहाक

Civil engineering	토목공학	थोमोक-खोंग-हाक
Computer engineering	컴퓨터공학	खम्फ्यूथअ-खोग-हाक
Domestic science	가정학	खाजंग-हाक
Economics	경제학	ख्यंग्जे-हाक
Education	교육학	ख्योयूक-हाक
Engineering	공학	खोंग-हाक
English	영어	यंगअ
Fashion	의류학	उइरयू-हाक
Geography	지리학	छीरी-हाक
Geology	지질학	छीजील-हाक
Grammar	문법	मुन्फप
History	국사	खुक्सा
Industrial engineering	산업공학	सानप-खोंग-हाक
IT engineering	정보통신학	छंग्बो थोंग्सीन-हाक
Law	법학	फप-हाक
Life science	생명과학	सेंग-म्यंग-ख्वाहाक
Linguistics	언어학	अनअ-हाक
Literature	문학	मुन-हाक
Mathematics	수학	सु-हाक
Mechanical engineering	기계공학	खिग्ये-खोंग-हाक
Medical science	의학	उई-हाक
Microbiology	미생물학	मिसेंग्मुल-हाक
Music	음악	उमाक
Nursing science	간호학	खान्हो-हाक
Pharmacy	약학	याक-हाक

Philosophy	철학	छल-हाक
Physical education	체육	छेयूक-हाक
Physics	물리	मुल्ली-हाक
Political science and diplomacy	정치외교학	छंग्छी वेग्यो-हाक
Politics	정치학	छंग्छी-हाक
Psychology	심리학	सिम्नी हाक
Science	과학	ख्वा-हाक
Sociology	사회학	साह्वे-हाक
Statistics	통계학	थोंग्यो-हाक
Tourism	관광학	ख्वान-ग्वांग-हाक
Veterinary medicine	수의학	सुई-हाक

PROFESSIONS

English	Hangeul	Pronunciation
Accountant	회계사	ह्वेग्येसा
Actor/actress	배우	फेउ
Archaeologist	고고학자	खोगोहाक्चा
Architect	건축가	खन्छुक्का
Barber	이용사	इयोंग्सा
Car mechanic	정비사	छंग्बीसा
Carpenter	목수	मोक्सू
Cartoonist	만화가	मान्ह्वागा
Chef	요리사	योरीसा
Clerk	사무원	सामूवन
Cook	조리사	छोरीसा
Dietitian	영양사	यंग्यांग्सा

Doctor	의사	उइसा
Driver	운전수	उन्जन्सू
Electrician	전기공	छन्गीगोंग
Engineer	기관사	खीग्वान्सा
Farmer	농부	नोंग्बू
Fashion designer	의상디자이너	उइसांग दीजाइनअ
Fisher	어부	अबू
Gardener	원예사	वन्येसा
Homemaker	주부	छूबू
Judge	판사	फान्सा
Lawyer	변호사	प्यन्होसा
Member of National Assembly	국회의원	खुख्वे उइवन
Newspaper publisher	신문편집인	सिन्मुन प्यन्छीबीन
Novelist	소설가	सोसल्गा
Nurse	간호사	खान्होसा
Painter	화가	ह्वागा
Photographer	사진가	साजीन्गा
Pilot	조종사	छोजोंग्सा
Player	연주가	यन्जूगा
Plumber	배관공	फेग्वान्गोंग
Police	경찰	ख्यंग्छाल
Postman	우체부	उछेबू
President	대통령	थेथोंग-न्यंग
Professor	교수	ख्योसू
Researcher	연구원	यन्गूवन
Salesperson	판매원	फान्मेवन

Scholar	학자	हाक्चा
Secretary	비서	फीसअ
Soldier	군인	खुनिन
Student	학생	हाक्सेंग
Teacher	교사	ख्योसा
Telephone operator	전화교환수	छान्हा ख्योहान्सू
Veterinarian	수의사	सूउइसा
Waiter	웨이터	वेइथअ
Writer	극작가	खुक्चाक्का

Airport

English	Hangeul	Pronunciation
Airline ticket	항공권	हांगोंग्वन
Airport	공항	खोंग-हांग
Airport immigration Office	출입국관리소	छुरीप्पुक-ख्वाल्लीसो
Arrival	도착	थोछाक
Arrival/departure card	출입국신고서	छुरीप्पुक सिन्गोसअ
Aviation	항공	हांगोंग
Baggage	수하물	सुहामुल
Boarding	탑승	थाप्सुंग
Boarding pass	탑승권	थाप्सुग्वान
Cancellation of air service	결항	ख्यर्हांग
Check-in counter	체크인카운터	छेखु-इन खाउन्थअ
Currency exchange	환전소	हान्जन्सो

Customs duties	관세	ख्वान्से
Customs inspection port	세관검색대	सेग्वान्गम सेक्ते
Customs official	세관원	सेग्वान-वन
delay	지연	छीयन
Departing from a country	출국	छुल्गुक
Departure	출발	छुल्बाल
Domestic air	국내선	खुंग्नेसन
Duty free shop	면세점	म्यन्सेजम
Entering a country	입국	इपकुक
gate	게이트	गेइथु
International air	국제선	खुक्चेसन
Lounge	라운지	राउन्जी
One-way	편도	फ्यन्दो
Passenger	탑승객	थाप्सुंग-गेक
Passenger terminal	여객터미널	योगेक थमिनल
Passport	여권	यग्वान
Passport inspection (Departure)	출국여권심사대	छुल्गुक यक्वन सिम्सादे
Passport inspection (entry)	입국여권심사대	इप्गुक यक्वन सिम्सादे
Return (round) trip	왕복	वांग्बोक
Route	노선	नोसन
Shipping service	운항	उन्हांग
Transfer	환승	हान्सुंग
Visa	비자	फीजा

Business / Service

English	Hangeul	Pronunciation
Accounting	회계	हेग्ये
Annual salary	연봉	यन्बोंग
Agriculture	농업	नोंग-अप
Bidding	입찰	इप्छाल
Bill	어음	अऊम
Bond	채권	छेग्वन
Bonus	상여금	सांग-यगुम
Business	사업	साअप
Business trip	출장	छुल्जांग
Capital	자본	छाबोन
Company	회사	हेसा
Contract	계약	ख्येयाक
Construction	건설업	खन्सल-अप
Cooperation/ partnership	제휴	छेह्यू
Corporation	주식회사	छूसीक-हेसा
Custom	관세	ख्वान्से
Debt	채무	छेमु
Debt/liabilities	부채	फूछे
Deficit	적자	छक्चा
Demand	수요	सुयो
Entering a company	입사	इप्सा
Enterprise	기업	खिअप
Export	수출	सुछुल
Export & import business	무역	मुयक

Financial affairs	재무	छेमु
Healthcare	보건업	फोगन-अप
Import	수입	सुइप
Income	소득	सोदुक
Investment	투자	थुजा
Information Techno-liogy	정보통신업	छंग्बो थोंग्सीन-अप
Large enterprise	대기업	थे-खिअप
License/patent	특허	थुखअ
Limited company	유한회사	यूहान-ह्वेसा
Loss	손해	सोन्हो
Lodging/hospitality	숙박업	सुक्पाक-अप
Management	경영	ख्यंग्यंग
Manufacture	제조	छेजो
Margin	마진	माजीन
Market	시장	सीजांग
Merger	합병	हाप्यंग
Monthly salary	월급	वल्गुप
Negotiation	협상	ह्याप्सांग
Pay	급여	खुप्यअ
Product	상품	सांग्फुम
Production	생산	सेंग्सान
Profit	이익	इइक
Property	자산	छासान
Purchase	구매	खुमे
Publishing	출판업	छुल्फान-अप
Real estate	부동산업	फोदोंग्सान-अप
Restaurant business	음식점업	उम्सीक्चम-अप

Retail business	소매업	सोमे-अप
Retirement	퇴직	थ्वेजिक
Sale	판매	फान्मे
Service business	서비스업	सबिसु-अप
Small- & medium-sized businesses	중소기업	छुंग्सो-खिअप
Stockholder	주주	छुजु
Supply	공급	खोंगुप
Transportation	운수업	उन्सु-अप
Tax	세금	सेगुम
Tax affairs	세무	सेमु
Trade	교역	ख्योयक
Trademark	상표	सांग्फ्यो
Undertaking	인수	इन्सु
Union	연합	यन्हाप
Wages	임금	इम्गुम
Wholesale business	도매업	धोमे-अप

Accessories

English	Hangeul	Pronunciation
Accessory	액세서리	एक्सेसरी
Jewel	보석	फोसक
Jewelry	귀금속	ख्वीगुम्सोक
Wristwatch	시계	सीग्ये
Bracelet	팔찌	फाल्ची
Earring	귀고리	ख्वीगोरी
Ring	반지	फान्जी
Necklace	목걸이	मोक-खरी
Pendant	펜던트	फेन्दंथु

Locket	로켓	रोखेथु
Necktie	넥타이	नेक-थाइ
Hair pin	머리핀	मरी-फिन
Headband	머리띠	मरी-त्ती
Key ring	열쇠고리	यल्स्वे खोरी
Hat	모자	मोजा
Ribbon	리본	रीबोन
Veil	베일	फेइल
Scarf	스카프	सुखाफु
Shawl	숄	शौल
Shoes	구두	खुदू
Footwear	신발	सिन्बाल
Sneakers	운동화	उन्दोंग-ह्वा
Socks	양말	यांग्माल
Belt	허리띠	हरी-त्ती
Gloves	장갑	छांगाप
Umbrella	우산	उसान
Fan	부채	फुछे
Handkerchief	손수건	सोन-सुगन
Glasses	안경	अन्यंग
Bag	가방	खाबांग
Purse	지갑	छीगाप

IT Related

English	Hangeul	Pronunciation
Access	접근/액세스	छप्कुन/एक्सेसु
Access log	액세스 로그	एक्सेसु लोगु
Ai (artificial intelligence)	인공지능	इंगोंग जीनुंग

Algorithm	알고리즘	आल्गोरीज़ुम
Analog	아날로그	आनाल्लोग
Apache	아파치	आफ़ाछी
Applet	애플릿	एफुल्लीत
Application	애플리케이션	एफुलीखेइशन
Array	배열	फेयल
Authoring tool	저작도구	छजाक थोगु
Backup	백업	फेगप
Bandwidth	대역폭	थेयक्पोक
Banner	배너	फेनअ
Benchmark	벤치마크	फेन्छीमाखु
Beta test	베타 테스트	फेथा थेसुधु
Bios (basic input/ output system)	기본 입출력 시스템	खीबोन इप्छुल्यक सीस्थेम
Bit map	비트맵	फीथुमेप
Blog (web log)	블로그	बुलोगु
Bookmark	북마크	बुक्माखु
Boot	부트	बुथु
Bootable floppy	부팅 디스켓	बूथिंग दिस्खेत
Bottleneck	병목 현상	फ्यंगमोक ह्यन्सांग
Broadcast	브로드캐스트	बुरोदुखेस्थु
Browser	브라우저	बफअ
Buffer	버퍼	बगु
Bug	버그	खेइबुत
Cable modem	케이블 모뎀	मोदेम
Cache	캐싱	खेसी

Cad (computer-aided design)	컴퓨터를 이용한 설계	खम्फ्यूथुल इयोंगहान सल्ग्ये
Card	카드	खादु
Celeron	셀러론	सेल्लरोन
Chatting	채팅/온라인 대화	छेथीग/ओन्लाइन थेह्य
Check box	채크박스	छेखुबाक्सु
Chip	칩	छीप
Chipset	칩셋	छीप्सेत
Class	클래스	ख्लेस
Click	클릭	खुलिक
Client	클라이언트	खुलाइन्थु
Clip art	클립아트/조각 그림	खुलिप आथु/छोगाक खुरीम
Clipboard	클립보드	खुलिप बोदु
Cluster	클러스터	खुलस्थअ
Codec (coder/decoder or compression/decompression)	코덱	खोदेक
Compiler	컴파일러	खम्फाइलअ
Component	컴포넌트	खम्फोनन्थु
Compression	(파일) 압축	(फाइल) आप्छुक
Computer	컴퓨터	खम्फ्यूथअ
Computer virus	컴퓨터 바이러스	खम्फ्यूथअ बाइलसु
Console	콘솔	खोन्सोल
Cookie	쿠키	खुखी
Counter	카운터	खाउन्थअ
CPU (central processing unit)	중앙처리장치	छुंगांग-छअरी-छांग्छी

Cursor	커서	खअसअ
Cyber	사이버	साइबअ
Cyberspace	사이버스페이스	साइबअ-सुफेइसु
Daemon	데몬	थेमोन
Data	데이터	देइथअ
Data modeling	데이터 모델링	देइथअ-मोथेलिंग
Database	데이터베이스	देइथअ-फेइसु
Debugging	디버깅	थीबअखिंग
Delphi	델파이	थेलफाइ
Desktop	바탕화면/데스크탑	फाथांग-हआ-म्य्न/ थेसुखुथाप
Device driver	장치 드라이버	छांग्छी-थराइन
DHTML (dynamic HTML)	다이내믹 HTML	दाइनेमीक
Dialog box	대화상자	थेहांग-सांगजा
Dial-up	다이얼 업	दाइल-अप
Digital signature	전자 서명	छअनजा-सअम्यंग
Directory	디렉토리	दीरेक-थोरी
Diskette (floppy disk)	디스켓/플로피 디스크	दीसुखेथ/फुल्लोफी-दीसुखु
Domain	도메인	थोमेइन
Download	내려받기/다운로드	नेल्फाथ्गी/थाउनलोदु
Drag	드래그/끌기	थुरेगु/क्लजी
Drive	구동장치/드라이브	खुदोंग-छांग्छी/दुराइबु
Driver	드라이버/구동 프로그램	दुराइबअ/खुदोंग-फरोगुरेम
E-business (electronic	전자상거래	छअन्छा-सांगरे

business)		
E-mail (electronic mail)	전자우편	छन्जा-उफ्यन
Engine	엔진	एन्जीन
Executable file	실행 파일	सीऱहेंग-फाइल
File	파일	फाइल
Firewall	방화벽	फांगह्वाब्यक
Flash	플래시	फ्लेसी
Folder	폴더	फोल्दअ
Font	폰트/글꼴	फोन्थु/खुलकोल
Format	포맷	फोमेथ
Freeware	프리웨어	फुरीवेअ
Function	함수	हाम्सू
GPU (graphics processing unit)	그래픽 처리 장치	खुरेफिक-छरी-छांगछी
Hacker	해커	हेखअ
Hard disk	하드디스크	हादु-दीसुख
Hardware	하드웨어	हादुवेय
Home page	홈 페이지	होम-फेइजी
Host	호스트	होस्थ
Hosting	(웹)호스팅	(बेब) होसुथिंग
Hot key	바로 가기 키/단축 키	फारो-खागी-खी/ थान-छुक्-खी
Hub	허브	हब
Hyperlink	하이퍼미디어	हाइफअलिंख
Hypermedia	하이퍼미디어	हाइफअ-मीदीअ

Hypertext	하이퍼텍스트	हाइफअ-थेक्सुथु
I/o (input/output)	입력/출력	ग्रन्यक/छुल्यक
Icon	아이콘	आइखोन
Image	이미지	इमीजी
Infranet	인프라넷	इनफ्रानेथ
Instruction	명령어	म्यंगन्यंगअ
Integrity	무결성	मुग्यल-संग
Interface	인터페이스	इन्थअ-फेइसु
Internet	인터넷	इनथअ-नेथ
Intranet	인트라넷	इन्थुरानेथ
Jaz drive	재즈 드라이브	छेजु-दुराइबु
Keyboard	키보드	खी-बोदु
Kiosk	키오스크	खीओसुखु
LAN (local area network)	근거리 통신망	खुनगअरि-थोंगसिनमांग
Laptop computer	랩톱 컴퓨터	लेपथोप-खमप्युथअ
Latency	지연 시간	छियन-सिगान
LCD (liquid crystal display)	액정화면	ऐकजंग-ह्वाम्यन
Link	링크	लिंख
Linux	리눅스	लिनुकसु
Literal	리터럴	लिथअरअल
Logon and login	로그온/로그인	लोगुओन/लोगुइन
Loop	루프/반복	लूफ/फानबोक
Macintosh	매킨토시	मेखि[illegible] थोसी
Mail server or mta (mail transfer agent)	메일서버	मेइल-सअबअ

Mailing list	메일링 리스트	मेइल्लिंग-लिसुथु
Main board	메인보드	मेइनबोदु
Mainframe	메인프레임	मेइन-फुरेइम
Memory	메모리	मेमोरी
Menu bar	메뉴 표시줄	मेन्यु-फ्योसीजुल
Meta tag	메타 태그	मेथा-थेगु
Method	메쏘드	मेथोदु
Microchip	마이크로칩	माइखुरोछीब
Microprocessor	마이크로프로세서	माइखुरो-फुरोसेसअ
Migration	마이그레이션	माइग्रेइस्यन
Mirror site	미러사이트	मीरअसाइथु
Mirroring	미러링	मीरअरींग
Modem (modulator /demodulator)	모뎀/변복조기	मोदेम/फ्यन-फोकजोगी
Module	모듈	मोद्यूल
Monitor	모니터	मोनीथअ
Motherboard	마더보드	मादुबोदु
Mouse	마우스	माउसु
Mozilla	모질라	मोजिल्ला
MSIE (microsoft internet explorer)	인터넷 익스플로러	इनथअनेथ-इक्सु-फुल्लोरअ
Multicast	멀티캐스트	मअल्थी-खेसुथु
Multimedia	멀티미디어	मअल्थी-मीदीअ
Multiprocessing	멀티프로세싱	मअल्थी-फुरोसेसींग
Name server	네임서버	नेइम-सअबअ
Netiquette	네티켓	नेथीखेथ
Netizen	네티즌	नेथीजन

Net mask	넷마스크	नेथमासुखु
Netscape	넷스케이프	नेथु-सुखेइफु
Network	네트웍	नेथु-वअक
Newsgroup	뉴스그룹	न्यूसु-गुरुप
NIC (network interface card)	네트웍 카드	नेथु-वअक-खादु
Node	노드	नोदु
Notebook computer	노트북 컴퓨터	नोथुबूक-खअमफ्यूथअ
Object	객체	खेकछे
Offline	오프라인	ओलफुलाइन
OS (operating system)	운영체계	उन्यंग-छेगे
Overlay	오버레이	ओबअलेइ
Packet	패킷	फेखिथ
Parameter	매개변수	मेगेब्यनसु
Partition	파티션/분할	फाथीस्यन/फूनहाल
Password	암호/패스워드	आम्हो/फेसुवअथु
Permission	퍼미션/(접근) 허가	फअमीस्यन/(छअपगुन) हअगा
Pixel	화소	ह्वासो
Pop-up	팝업	फाबअप
Port	포트	फोथु
Portal/portal site	포탈/포탈 사이트	फोथाल/फोथाल साइथु
Printer	프린터	फुरीन्थु
Process	프로세스	फुरोसेसु
Processor	프로세서	फुरोसेसअ
Query	쿼리/질의	खुअरी/छिरे

RAM (random access memory)	램	रेम
Real time and real-time	실시간	सील्गीगान
Redirector	리다이렉터	री-दारेख्थअ
Register	레지스터	रेजिसुथअ
Registry	레지스트리	रेजिसुथुरी
Resolution	해상도	हेसांग्दो
Resource	자원/리소스	छावअन/रिसोसु
Ripper	리퍼	रीफअ
Roaming service	로밍 서비스	रोमींग-सअबिसु
Rollover	롤오버	रोलोबअ
ROM (read-only memory)	롬	रोम
Router	라우터	राउथअ
Routine and subr outine	루틴과 서브 루틴	रूथीन-ग्वा-सअबुरुथिन
Routing table	라우팅 테이블	रूथिंग-थेइबुल
Runtime	런타임	रअन्थाइम
Safe mode	안전모드	आन्जअन-मोदु
Screen saver	화면보호기	ह्वाम्यन-फोहोगी
Screen shot	스크린샷/ 화면갈무리	सुखुरिनस्याथ/ह्वाम्यन-खालमुरी
Scroll	스크롤	सुखुरोल
Semiconductor	반도체	फान्दोछे
Serial	직렬/시리얼	छींगन्यल/सीरीअल
Server	서버	सअबअ
Service pack	서비스 팩	सअबीसु-फेक

Set-top box	셋톱박스	सेथ-थोप-बाक्सु
Shareware	셰어웨어	सेअवेअ
Shortcut	단축 아이콘	थानछुक-आइखोन
Site	사이트	साइथु
Snapshot	스냅샷	सुनेप-स्याथ
Software	소프트웨어	सोफुथुवेअ
Solution	솔루션	सोल्लुस्यन
Sound card	사운드 카드	साउन्दु-खादु
Spam (junk e-mail)	스팸	सुफेम
Spy ware	스파이웨어	सुफाइवेअ
Static ip address/ Dynamic IP address	고정 IP 주소/유동 IP 주소	खोजंग आइ पी छुसो/यूथोंग आइ पी छुसो
String	스트링/문자열	सुथुरिंग/मुन्जायल
Subnet and subnet mask	서브넷과 서브넷 마스크	सअबुनेथ ग्वा सअबुनेथ मासुखु
Surfing	(웹)써핑	(वेब) सअफिंग
Sysop (system operator)	시삽	सिसाप
System	시스템	सीसुथेम
Table	테이블	थेइबुल
Tag	태그	थेगु
Task/multitasking	태스크/멀티태스킹	थेसुखु/मअल्थी-थेसुखींग
Telnet	텔넷/원격접속	थेलनेथ/वअनख्यक-छअप्सो
Terminal	단말기/터미널	थानमालगी/ थअमीनअल

Terminal server	터미널 서버	थअमीनअल-सअबअ
Text	텍스트	थेकसुथु
Thread/multi threading	스레드/멀티스레딩	सुरेथु/मअल्थी-सुरेथिंग
Tool tip	도구 도움말	थोगु-थो-उम्माल
Toolbar	툴바	थूलबा
Track	트랙	थुरेक
Uncompressing	압축풀기	आप्छुक-फूल्गी
Upgrade	업그레이드	अपगुरेइदु
Upload	올려주기/업로드	ओल्यछूगी/अप्लोदु
Utility	유틸리티	यूथिलिथी
Video adapter	그래픽카드	खुरेफिक-खादु
Virtual memory	가상 메모리	खासांग-मेमोरी
Virtual reality	가상 현실	खासांग-ह्यनसिल
Visual basic	비주얼 베이직	फीजुअल-फेइजिक
Web mail (web-based e-mail)	웹메일	वेबमेइल
Web server	웹서버	वेब-सअबअ
Fibro (wireless broadband)	와이브로	वाइबूरो
Window	윈도우	विन्दो-उ
Wireless	무선	मुसअन
Wireless lan (wireless local area network)	©무선 랜	मुसअन-रेन
WWW (world wide web)	월드와이드웹	वअल्दु-वाइदु-वेब

♦ ♦ ♦

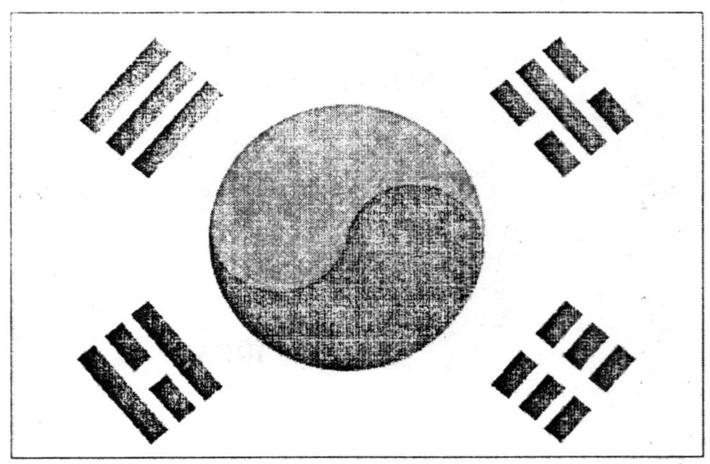

SOUTH KOREAN FLAG "THAE-GEUKKI"

The flag of South Korea is called "Thae-geukki" which symbolizes the thought, philosophy, and mysticism of the Far East in general and Korea in particular.

There are combinations of three unbroken and broken bars - around the *taegeuk* circle. The circle in the center, upper half and lower half, represents absolute, or the essential unity of men and nature. The *Yang* (positive) and the *Yin* (negative) divisions within the circle represent duality like night and day, fire and water, life and death or good and evil.

The four trigrams of the flag also indicate the duality of opposites and balances. In the upper right trigram, two broken lines separated by an unbroken line is the symbol of Water; opposite to them is Fire, symbolized by two unbroken lines separated by a broken line. In the upper left trigram, three unbroken lines symbolize Heaven; opposite to them in the lower right are all three broken lines which represent Earth.

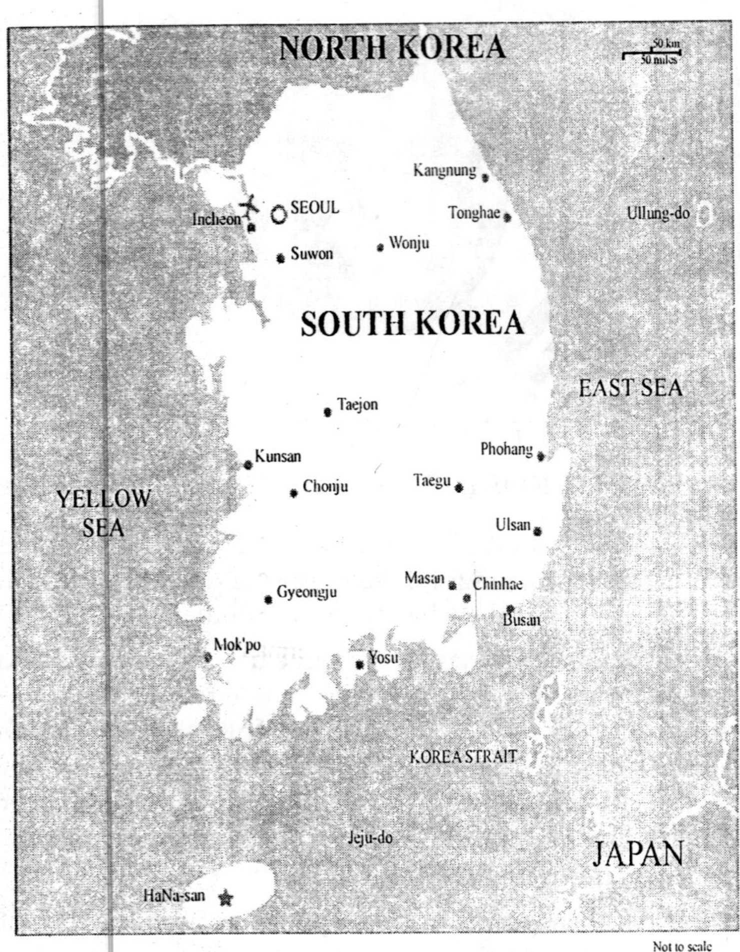
NORTH KOREA
50 km
50 miles
Kangnung
SEOUL
Incheon
Tonghae
Ullung-do
Suwon
Wonju
SOUTH KOREA
EAST SEA
Taejon
Kunsan
Phohang
Chonju
Taegu
YELLOW SEA
Ulsan
Masan
Chinhae
Gyeongju
Busan
Mok'po
Yosu
KOREA STRAIT
Jeju-do
JAPAN
HaNa-san
Not to scale

Other Books on
LANGUAGE BOOKS

1. Learn to Speak and Write Arabic
2. Teach Yourself Spanish
3. Learn to Speak and Write Russian
4. Learn to Speak and Write Korean
5. French Made Easy
6. Learn to Speak and Write Hindi
7. Learn to Speak and Write Italian
8. Conversational Chinese
9. Learn to Speak and Write French
10. Learn to Speak and Write German
11. Learn to Speak and Write Spanish
12. Learn to Speak and Write Japanese